# Thirty Days With Abraham Lincoln

# Quiet Fire

## Duncan Newcomer

Front Edge Publishing

For more information and further discussion, visit

**www.ThirtyDaysWith.com**

**www.DuncanNewcomer.com**

Copyright © 2019 by Duncan Newcomer
All Rights Reserved
ISBN: 978-1-64180-054-9
Version 1.0

Author photo by Susan S. Crysler

Cover design by Rick Nease
www.RickNeaseArt.com

Quiet Fire audio archive provided by WERU Community Radio
http://weru.org
https://archives.weru.org/category/quiet-fire/

Abraham Lincoln, head-and-shoulders portrait, sourced from the United
States Library of Congress, public domain and available at:
https://commons.wikimedia.org/wiki/File:Gardner-Photo-Lincoln.jpg

Published by
Front Edge Publishing, LLC
42807 Ford Road, Suite 234
Canton, Michigan

Front Edge Publishing specializes in speed and flexibility in adapting
and updating our books. We can include links to video and other
online media. We offer discounts on bulk purchases for special events,
corporate training, and small groups. We are able to customize bulk
orders by adding corporate or event logos on the cover and we can
include additional pages inside describing your event or corporation. For
more information about our fast and flexible publishing or permission
to use our materials, please contact Front Edge Publishing at info@
FrontEdgePublishing.com.

# Contents

This book is dedicated to my great-uncle, James Duncan, who was born in County Londonderry, Northern Ireland, on September 5, 1843, and died in a Union hospital in Danville, Kentucky, on November 8, 1862, from wounds to his hip and from measles.

James was a boy of piety, signing all his letters with, "Remember me to all my friends and give my love to all my brothers and sister and when you bow before the Mercy Seat remember your soldier boy."

James was also patriotic, signing up with Illinois Company I, 80th Regiment in the summer of 1862, following President Lincoln's call for additional troops. Southern Illinois was a Democratic territory, but it exceeded in numbers the mandated call.

# Praise for *Quiet Fire*

Since its beginning, radio has offered a warm medium for connecting the heart, the head, and the imagination. This delightful collection of Lincoln's wisdom was seeded in a creative radio show, *Quiet Fire*. It has morphed into a daily companion for readers who connect the dots between time and space to map a new understanding of the chaotic times in which we live. Lincoln's words resonate more urgently than ever, and Duncan has played alchemist in *Quiet Fire* to one of our country's greatest souls and distilled an essence that can guide and comfort us.

**Sally Kane,** *CEO, National Federation of Community Broadcasters.*

This book is full of surprise and insight, head-scratching thoughts and images that will linger in your mind beyond the thirty days. In each of the *Thirty Days With Abraham Lincoln*, Duncan Newcomer humbly asks his readers to contemplate a great thought from a great man, to sit staring into a *Quiet Fire*. Between Lincoln's wisdom and Newcomer's insights the reader will wish the month had many more days.

**Brian "Fox" Ellis,** *author, storyteller and historical re-enactor who portrays seven 'Friends of Lincoln'.*

As Lincoln himself did, these words cast a healing and inspiriting spell. In a time when we have all but forgotten what a leader is—what a hero is—Duncan Newcomer's stories help restore to us a wise and compassionate leader. Listen to these 30 reflections one at a time, read them, or listen and read all at once. They will change your life in a subtle way, quiet you, restore calm and wisdom. But they will change you.

**The Rev. Dr. Eileen Sypher,** Emeritus Professor of English at George Mason University.

A timely echo of Lincoln's voice—to remind us of what Americans, at their best, aspire to be.

**Richard S. Slotkin,** *author of* Abe: A Novel of the Young Lincoln.

Once again, we are a nation at war within ourselves regarding what it means to be an American and questioning our most important founding values. *Thirty Days With Abraham Lincoln: Quiet Fire* is a powerful and important book that ... inspires us to reclaim the values essential for putting our house in order once again.

**Dr. John Oliver Wilson,** *Founder-Director of the Idea of America Network for the Colonial Williamsburg Foundation.*

These are elegant, meditative reflections inspired by America's most admired president. Duncan Newcomer's Lincoln still transcends transactional politics and regularly reminds us, by his example and words, of America's higher aspirations.

**Thomas E. Cronin,** *President Emeritus of Whitman College and author of* Imagining A Great Republic: Political Novels and the Idea of America.

Through the words and life of Abraham Lincoln, Duncan Newcomer conveys with passion and erudition how much the Great Emancipator has to teach us. Yes, more books have been written about Lincoln than anyone besides Jesus Christ, but from his famous "mystic chords of memory" there probably aren't that many that have coaxed such intriguing and inspiring notes.

**David Margolick,** *author of* The Promise and the Dream: The Untold Story of Martin Luther King, Jr. and Robert F. Kennedy.

These healing, inspiring readings are especially welcome in the gloomy present context of our nation's politics.

**Dave Edgerton,** *author of the novel* 270 East.

We invite you to join this "spiritual conversation" with Abraham Lincoln, surely one of our most revered presidents. Through Lincoln's words we can reflect on this crisis of values in our nation today and still be guided by this remarkable man. We have found this book a fitting addition to our own daily routine of prayer and meditation and highly commend it to you.

**Ray and Patricia Estabrook,** *founders and directors of the Game Loft, a youth development program that has promoted Positive Youth Development for over 20 years.*

This book brings together the spiritual and the political, which was so much the essence of Lincoln—freedom's cause had to be carried out in history, in a political system. As the author notes, Lincoln found a way to do this without "ambition corrupting honor." It's a lesson in power to us. Want to return to a better picture of ourselves and our national identity? This is your book—a wonderful collection of short daily essays that is just plain restorative.

*William B. Bonvillian, MIT lecturer and author.*

Duncan Newcomer writes well, fluently, from the heart. His life-long dedication to Lincoln has been an anchor for his life and mind. It's an aspirational American story, both Duncan's and Lincoln's. Like all spiritual extrapolations, it has the advantage of its aspirational and idealistic resonances. The "spiritual" doesn't have the same meaning for me, that it has for Duncan. Still, what Duncan has done, and is doing, will be helpful to many people.

*Fred Kaplan, author of* The Biography of a Writer: Lincoln.

Duncan Newcomer gives us the gift of Abraham Lincoln's wise words and Duncan's own thoughtful reflections on a side of the great president most of us have not really seen. Read this book every day for a month, and you will not only be heartened and enlightened but also given hope for our own troubled times.

*Sheryl Fullerton, retired Executive Editor for Religion & Spirituality at John Wiley & Sons, Inc.*

Duncan Newcomer understands that life has its natural rhythms. After reading the thirty selections for these daily devotionals, it is a testament to Dr. Newcomer's mastery that he was able to perfectly curate the mass of Lincoln's writings into concise lessons that resonate all day.

*Gary Dickson, author of* An Improbable Pairing.

Oh, that we had an Abraham Lincoln today! Now, we do have Abraham Lincoln's words and deeds, and Duncan Newcomer's trenchant accounting of what lay behind those words and deeds.

*Jeff Byrum, radio listener, choral singer and retired IT engineer.*

# Foreword

By Peter M. Wallace

When Father's Day approached each year when I was young, I knew what I would get my dad: I'd visit a bookstore in search of a new book on Lincoln. One year it was one of many tomes on Lincoln in the Civil War. Another year I gave him Quaker theologian Elton Trueblood's book, *The Spiritual Pilgrimage of Abraham Lincoln*. He particularly liked that one.

In his preacher study, my dad kept a life-size bronze bust of Lincoln, which brooded over his shoulder as he prepared sermons. Dad's library of Lincolniana, collected through the years (and not just from me) was quite sizable; he enjoyed delving into it from time to time.

When I was a teenager in West Virginia, a large bronze sculpture entitled "Abraham Lincoln Walks at Midnight" was installed on the state capitol grounds in 1969. This powerful image had been commissioned to celebrate (though belatedly) the centennial of West Virginia's statehood. In 1863, in the midst of the Civil War, Lincoln carved my home state's odd boundary along the Allegheny Mountains from the mother state of Virginia. The statue was criticized at the time, as I recall, because Lincoln appeared so dreadfully melancholy—and hopefully not because of the new state he'd created. But I think it captured Lincoln's demeanor during that awful time in our history in a graceful, powerful way.

So Abraham Lincoln made a sizable impression on my life from a young age. And not mine only—Lincoln routinely tops all the favorite president polls. There's good reason for this.

Now, Duncan Newcomer has added to the Lincoln library, and how I wish I could gift this book to my father. He would relish it. I certainly do, and I am confident you will too.

Duncan captures Lincoln's spirit in every one of these thirty meditations, each springboarded by a potent quote by Lincoln or someone who knew him. (I love the fact that these began life as radio essays since I am a radio guy as well.)

By reading these sublime and soulful reflections, possessed (as Duncan puts it) by a quiet fire, you will find inspiration and insight that will make sense in your own life, in your own battles with fear and grief, in your own decisions over the best path to take in a certain situation, in your own yearning for deep meaning and purpose.

As an author of spiritual meditations myself, I am thrilled by this first in a new series of "Thirty Days With …" books from Front Edge Publishing. What a powerful concept for today's readers who are so bombarded by electronic messages of all kinds from all sides: to simply take a few minutes each day to read and ponder and question and enjoy. This book, focusing so winsomely on the spiritual wisdom of the sixteenth president, will help you launch a life-changing practice you will want to continue.

In his introduction Duncan references the "Wide Awakes," a movement of young men and women who supported Lincoln for president. Today we talk about being "woke" to the needs of our fellow human beings around us. Lincoln remains a powerful guide for us. As Duncan writes, "Lincoln himself certainly was a Wide Awake, awake to the fire within him connected to the fire he believed enlightened America." Through these meditations, Lincoln's spirit can continue to inspire us—to keep us "woke."

In these pages you will occasionally run into the magnificent American poet Walt Whitman, which is fitting indeed. Just recently I read a quotation by Whitman about Lincoln that strikingly captures his essence:

> "See how he went his own lonely road, disregarding all the usual ways—refusing the guides, accepting no warnings: just keeping his appointment with himself every time." [1]

Now I encourage you to keep an appointment with Lincoln as well for thirty days, and watch what might become of your faith, your spirit, your dedication to justice and peace, your purpose.

I believe you will be amazed.

—Peter M. Wallace is the producer and host of the nationally syndicated radio program and podcast, "Day1" (Day1.org), an Episcopal priest, and author/editor of 12 books including *The Passionate Jesus* and *Heart and Soul: The Emotions of Jesus.*

---

1  Brenda Wineapple, editor. *Walt Whitman Speaks: His Final Thoughts on Life, Writing, Spirituality, and the Promise of America as Told to Horace Traubel* (New York: Library of America, 2019) 14.

# Preface

by John Burt

In the last of these 30 meditations, Duncan Newcomer describes how visitors at the Lincoln Memorial in Washington DC often linger at that site—returning to gaze at Daniel Chester French's magnificent large seated sculpture of the martyred Lincoln, or silently to read the words of the Gettysburg and Second Inaugural Address carved into the inner walls of that great Doric temple. Perhaps they also pause at that place on the front steps of the building where Martin Luther King delivered the "I Have a Dream" speech in August, 1963, and where Marian Anderson, refused permission for racist reasons to sing at Constitution Hall, would sing on Easter Sunday in 1939 for an integrated audience in that then-still-segregated city. To invoke King and Anderson is also in a way to invoke Lincoln, whose special calling was to face—and to face down—the legacy of slavery and racism in this country and to lead the United States in its first few halting steps towards racial equality.

During his First Inaugural Address, when Lincoln invoked "the better angels of our nature," he had in mind something historical and national, but also something personal and moral. He was calling for some stay against confusion and issuing a reminder of better possibilities. This is the Lincoln we have turned toward repeatedly in the years since his death, never more perhaps than in the distracted present, in which his message of reconciliation, particularly of racial reconciliation, has taken on a new urgency.

George Washington has largely become an idea to Americans, the face in the Gilbert Stuart painting or the mythic figure in Parson Weems' fable. Even Thomas Jefferson, who seems to have dreamed up the main themes of American politics in an upstairs room in 1776, has faded into the promises he made for his country but was himself never quite able to keep. But Lincoln, unlike Washington and Jefferson, is pre-eminently and first of all an actual human being, someone one knows as one knows one's parents, not as one knows historical or biographical facts. What all those tourists seek, what Anderson and King sought, is to be with Lincoln, to correct and reframe and recover themselves and their country by getting right with him. They search for a vivifying reconnection to the promise and challenge of American life. But, more even than this, what they seek is communion with and living moral intimacy with the man Abraham Lincoln, as if by keeping faith one on one with that historical person one could become a better American and America a better America.

What Duncan Newcomer has provided in this book is not just thirty meditations upon Lincoln's life and thought, but thirty ways of being in his personal presence. Here we move in the landscapes of his childhood and youth, the fields and woods of Kentucky and Indiana, and the rivers— the Sangamon and the Illinois, the Ohio and the Mississippi—that rolled through them. We breathe his air and listen to the pitch and timbre of his voice, as if we were among those friends he led or challenged. We meditate with him on the lessons he learned as a local militia leader during the Black Hawk war or as a self-taught attorney on a rural circuit. We draw closer to him in his love of Nancy Hanks, his angel mother, and Sarah Johnston, his loving stepmother, and Ann Rutledge, the beloved of his youth. But most of all, the book seeks to put us in his presence as what Allen Guelzo famously called the Redeemer President, which is to say, in the presence of the liberator and war leader who gave our country its difficult and still incomplete second birth.

Duncan Newcomer pays the most acute attention to the ways in which Lincoln reconciled oppositions in his person, fusing and transcending gravity and levity, masculine and feminine, national and universal, justice and mercy. Most of all, he casts light on that central mystery which draws the imagination to Lincoln, his ability to fight a great war while resisting the temptation to hate his enemy, his ability to hold in one hand the necessity of reconciliation with his enemy and the necessity of liberating and protecting those the enemy sought to subject. He sees Lincoln's task was as much a spiritual one as a political one, one that requires but also enlists the deepest resources of the spirit.

This is a book of reflections, informed by a lifetime of reading and scholarship about Lincoln, and also by a lifetime of immersion in the moral and spiritual work of a counselor and clergyman. But it is also a book of meditations, of invitations to a first-person experience of communion with and through Lincoln, a kind of momentary sabbath at the heart of the everyday. It is an invitation to a habit of spiritual practice appropriate to the broken soul of this almost chosen people, as they seek to repair, and perhaps ultimately to perfect, this last best hope of earth.

—John Burt is Paul E. Prosswimmer Professor of American Literature at Brandeis University. He is the author of *Lincoln's Tragic Pragmatism* (2013).

# Introduction

IF GANDHI IS the Great Soul of India, the Mahatma, then Abraham Lincoln is America's Great Soul.

To this day, Lincoln's spirit soars far beyond the boundaries of the United States to inspire men and women around the world. More books have been written about Abraham Lincoln—at least 15,000—than about any other figure in world history, except Jesus. In Washington D.C., at the Ford's Theatre Center for Education and Leadership, some of those books are displayed in a towering bookshelf that stands 34 feet tall and 8 feet around the base. That's a mountain of books—about a mountain of a man.

That's why our team of writers and editors at Front Edge Publishing chose to inaugurate this new series of books of daily inspirational readings with a volume that explores Lincoln's spiritual wisdom day by day.

The idea of daily readings as a spiritual practice dates back thousands of years to Jewish cycles of readings and prayers. Christians and Muslims both adopted the idea of fixed-hour prayers, then various daily disciplines arose from that tradition. The Reformation was fueled by pamphleteers who urged regular religious reading in every community. In the early 20th century, Frances Craig, a Methodist laywoman in Texas, responded to the devastation of the Great Depression by organizing the distribution of daily inspirational readings through her church. By 1935, she was collaborating with a Methodist evangelist, the Rev. Grover Emmons, in the nationwide debut of *The Upper Room* magazine, offering a nonsectarian collection of daily readings for Christian families. The idea was so successful that other collections of daily readings followed. In 1956, a radio evangelist in Michigan launched a more evangelical series of daily texts, called Our Daily Bread. By the 1990s, the idea seemed passé. A long list of major publishers turned down the idea of a new, broad based series of uplifting books, called *Chicken Soup for the Soul*. Jack Canfield and Mark Hansen eventually partnered with a tiny Florida publishing house that was willing to take a risk on their idea that these short stories would find an audience. A quarter of a century later, the 250 Chicken Soup titles have sold more than 100 million copies.

# Expanding the Circle

In the 21st century, it's time to further expand the circle. One in four Americans now tell pollsters they don't have a religious affiliation. Americans now draw inspiration from a wide range of figures and cultures. In fact, with powerfully connected computers in the palms of their hands, Americans are reaching around the planet for sources of daily encouragement. Millions of us, even many devout Christian evangelicals, find solace in the Indian practices of yoga, for example. Millions of Americans meditate in practices that stem from Buddhism.

As the circle enlarges in this new millennium, we also have an opportunity to dig deeper into our collective human heritage on this planet. In this age of 24/7 news—from social media to news networks—millions have simply forgotten the inspirational riches of our past. When asked by pollsters, half of Americans can't name the four Gospels. Pollsters also regularly report that most of us can't recall basic details about the Civil War era—a defining part of our heritage. In fact, less than one in five Americans know that it was Lincoln's Emancipation Proclamation that ended slavery.

So, how do we reconnect with the rich wisdom of our collective heritage? No one wants to tackle that 34-foot-tall tower of books about Lincoln. Few of us have time to organize a personalized reading plan to explore the wisdom of great sages.

Instead, we are asking busy readers: Would you like an easy way to start each day with an uplifting reading? Would you enjoy a handy, 30-day sample of wisdom coupled with thoughtful questions to ponder? This idea of daily inspiration has been part of our religious DNA for thousands of years. Each morning, we could tap into those deep roots for encouragement. Over time with these new volumes, we could sample a range of great sages. As we read, we would discover encouraging anecdotes, quotes and ideas to share with friends. That's the impulse behind the millions of copies of inspirational readers that Americans have enjoyed over the past century—an idea now expanded to embrace a more diverse community of spiritual guides.

# A Popular Idea with an Eager Audience

So, we start this adventure with 30 days featuring the enduring wisdom of Abraham Lincoln. We know this will be popular, because this idea already has found an eager audience through a regional radio station in Maine.

As the creator of this Lincoln series, and this first "Thirty Days With" volume, I admit that there were skeptics as we launched this project.

"Spiritual meditations about Lincoln—broadcast on secular radio?" That's the incredulous question I faced when I first proposed the idea to the manager of WERU, a noncommercial community radio station founded in 1988, thanks to early support by Paul Stookey of Peter, Paul and Mary.

"This could be very popular," I said. "I want to call the series Quiet Fire. It's a program giving listeners quick, fascinating pieces on the spiritual life of Abraham Lincoln and its relevance to us today."

"And, why call it Quiet Fire?"

I told a story. I began, as I begin most of my radio broadcasts, with an invitation to spend a few minutes with me. I do that by offering a fun fact, a memorable quote. My introduction is a friendly offer to the audience: "Here's a Lincoln quote for you." Then, the quote I offered to explain the proposed series was this: "The fiery trial through which we pass will light us down in honor or dishonor to the latest generation."

That was how Abraham Lincoln closed his address to Congress on December 1, 1862. Our nation was in a crisis. People were angry and uncertain about a seemingly endless war. Lincoln's political party, the Republicans, had almost lost control of Congress. The other party, the Democrats, had gained greatly in recent elections. Many people in the north were very unhappy with the idea that freedom for slaves was now becoming a rationale for the war. This war had been, most thought, a conflict to preserve the union—and now Lincoln's Emancipation Proclamation was about to be officially issued on January 1, 1863.

As our nation's leaders thought about Lincoln's message, they wondered: What is this honor—or dishonor—that he so boldly insists will become our legacy? They realized the real question was: Do we have it within ourselves to save the union—and end slavery at the same time?

These were defining challenges for America and their answers would become their honor or their dishonor.

Lincoln put it bluntly: "In the giving of freedom to the slave we assure freedom to the free." It was a win-win in his mind, and it was now a moral choice for all Americans. Slavery not only enslaved blacks; it deeply bonded whites to cruelty and an ignoble, un-American way of life.

Lincoln believed that the fiery trials through which we pass forge our character. "No personal significance or insignificance can spare one or another of us," he said.

I've named this series of radio broadcasts "Quiet Fire" because those two words capture something essential about Abraham Lincoln and his spiritual life. Putting these two words together, quiet and fire, may seem contradictory. Not all fires are quiet, by any means. In fact, Lincoln was the Commander in Chief over America's greatest explosion of firepower to date—the Civil War.

Lincoln was full of contradictions, such as his rollicking humor that also was intimately acquainted with grief. In fact, his union of opposites is one of his paramount characteristics. You can hardly say one thing about Lincoln without having to then say the opposite. Just think of his face. People often said he was ugly—yet we have photographs and witnesses who speak of a calm and radiant beauty to his countenance. We often see Lincoln in our own artistic imagination as a boy, reading on the hearth, before the fire in the log cabin. More likely he read by candle light off in a corner or in a sleeping loft. It was a crowded cabin, maybe 14 by 16 feet, filled with a blended family of seven people. Among his many roles, Lincoln also was the candle keeper for the Free Baptist Church his parents attended. A little rolled-up note has been found between logs in the church, a scrap of paper on which he put down the sum of the candles remaining and signed it, as he did, A. Lincoln.

Fires and flames define Lincoln. One fiery flame he would have seen as a boy was the controlled burning of giant trees, the primeval forest of southern Indiana. To clear them for farmland, they would be girdled with an axe one year and then, dry and dead, set on fire the next. You can imagine this intelligent, sensitive boy watching these huge torches burning, fires by night, pillars of smoke by day. It must have reminded him of great fires in the Bible, including Moses' burning bush, setting the ancient patriarch on a course to call out: "Let my people go!"

The famous Catholic monk Thomas Merton once said, "Our spiritual and mystical destiny is to awake to the fire that is within us, and our happiness depends on the harmony-in-conflict that results from this awakening." True peace is the "hidden attunement of opposite tensions."

When Lincoln ran for the presidency, there was a popular youth movement that supported him. These young people would organize torchlight parades at night, the young men and women hoisting signs about freedom. They were called the "Wide Awakes." And, Lincoln himself certainly was a Wide Awake, awake to the fire within him connected to the fire he believed enlightened America. Abraham Lincoln's spirit continues to teach and to inspire us to this day.

## A Yonder Spirit

Lincoln would not have understood our contemporary phrase, "spiritual but not religious," because in his lifetime he was both—in his way. Lincoln was uneasy with religious beliefs and church membership, although he praised the churches in the Union for their support and he attended services regularly as an adult and as president. But he was reliant primarily on reason and was inspired by Jefferson's own more secular approach to enlightenment.

Key to Lincoln's spiritual life was a vision and a yearning so large that it could span the continent and encircle the world—a sense of yonder. Lincoln, a trained surveyor, said that there "is no line" that could be drawn between the slave world and the free. Like his great admirer Walt Whitman, Lincoln had a mystical idea of America. That idea of yonder was brought to Lincoln's story by his biographer Carl Sandburg, who associates it first with Abraham's mother Nancy Hanks. She would read or recite portions of scripture to young Abe that evoked this sense of a larger world, a larger calling. Historian-novelist Richard Slotkin describes the biblical passages rising up off the page as Hanks recounted the revelations and courage of Moses. As Slotkin describes the scene: "Abe leaned back in the warm swaddling, the bony curve of Mam's body, home-solid behind him, the river flowing under them all, dark and him drifting with it, yearning toward a dim shore that almost had a shape."

As these forces came together and were embodied in his life, Lincoln himself became a prophet who cried out for a balance that could keep our house from dividing—that could keep our nation from collapsing. So, to this day, people want to hear his wisdom. We know this because we hear from our radio listeners who tune in each Wednesday morning to WERU to hear a few more minutes of this series.

The on-air feature—which you can hear by following the links through-out this book to audio files archived by WERU—opens with words of welcome and a few bars of music from Czech composer Antonin Dvořák's New World Symphony. Dvořák composed this well-known work during his sojourn in the United States, from 1892 to 1895, as director of the National Conservatory of Music in New York City. His express purpose for the three-year visit was not to interpret European composers for the American public. "That is not my work and I would not waste any time on it. I came to discover what young Americans had in them and to help them express it."

The passage I excerpt for both the opening and closing of my broad-casts comes from the symphony's second movement, which is built around the beautiful "Comin' Home" theme. Assumed by many to be based on an American folk song, the theme was actually composed by Dvořák to demonstrate the inspiration of American sounds and traditions.

That's also an appropriate theme to close this introduction. We hope you will discover this new "Thirty Days With" series is calling you home—calling you to recognize your own connections with our human family. We welcome inquiries about group orders of these books, if you care to enjoy them with friends or a class or an entire community. Interested in the possibility of public appearances by our authors? Email us and share your ideas at info@FrontEdgePublishing.com.

We also welcome news about how this volume has touched your life—and your suggestions for future volumes.

Welcome to our community.

*Duncan Newcomer and the Front Edge Publishing team, Autumn 2019*

This is an example of a QR code, used throughout the book to link you directly to the archived broadcasts that inspired each chapter. To use it, download a free QR scanner application from your device's app store, or follow the provided short URL. These links will play recordings of the original broadcasts. You may notice that occasional references have been changed for the book. The QR code above links to the full archive of broadcasts at https://archives.weru.org/category/quiet-fire/

I

# 'Boys, Now I've Got You!'

*"Boys, now I've got you!"*

**-Abraham Lincoln**

http://bit.ly/2jBfgHq

"**BOYS, NOW I'VE** got you" doesn't sound too spiritual, does it? Yet Lincoln gleefully surprised his young friends in southern Indiana one day with these very words—words not found etched on the walls of the Lincoln Memorial.

But who were these boys Lincoln had gotten? We only know the name of one of them for sure—Joseph C. Richardson—because he told the story years later.

Lincoln may have cut a lonely figure out there on the American frontier, but he was, in fact, part of a community called Gentryville in Little Pigeon Creek. He had lots of friends, too. Within a mile of the Lincoln cabin there were nine families with a total of 49 children, and within five miles there were four times as many families.

But he figured out who was stealing melons from the Lincoln farm, and he knew just where they'd be headed as they stole away with the melons.

Now, I've lived in southern Indiana, and the melons there are pretty famous. Today they're called Posey County melons, though we'd call them cantaloupes—albeit big ones.

But, back to Lincoln. What do you suppose he did after he'd caught his friends melon-handed? Well, according to Joe Richardson, he cracked a few jokes and then sat down with them and joined in eating some of the contraband melons.

It is most likely that by this time, Lincoln was already over 6 feet tall and all big bones and muscle. It is highly likely that those young thieves never forgot being caught—and most likely that they never tried it again. Yet it is more than Lincoln's powerful enforcement that these youngsters probably remembered most; you'd expect that they also always recalled how he let them off easy—and, even more astonishingly, how he'd joined them in sharing the fruits of their crime! Through his actions, Lincoln converted these young people from petty criminals to common friends.

The melon-thief story is a parable—a story teaching a spiritual lesson. Lincoln had a heart for such unique generosity: It was one of his spiritual values. Lincoln would often affirm people and then deal generously with them, even when those people would try to steal from him—like when South Carolina tried to "steal" the American Union by attempting to secede from the nation.

We can wonder how Abraham Lincoln became so generous of heart. Perhaps it is because he had a strong, kind and gentle mother, followed by an extraordinary stepmother who held together a very divided house. But Lincoln also had books—books that taught him lessons. In school, Lincoln learned to read aloud with the rest of his classmates. The school that Lincoln attended was actually called a blab school, or vocal school, and as a result of this schooling Lincoln did most of his private reading out loud all his life!

At school, one of Lincoln's readers was called *Murray's English Reader*. Here are two quotes that were bred into Lincoln's bones by the time he caught his melon-thief friends:

"Revenge dwells in little minds."

"To have your enemy in your power, and yet to do him good, is the greatest heroism."

Now, Lincoln knew that he did not have a little mind. Therefore, revenge was not for him. But even more to the point of this spiritual virtue—both in how he dealt with his young friends and how he dealt with the southern states as the Civil War ended—is the second quote. Doing good by others is how Lincoln treated his friends, and it is also how he treated the South.

Lincoln certainly caught the South "stealing" the country. He was a hero not because his cause won the war, but because he planned to do good by the opposition.

Abraham Lincoln was a spiritual man, and his spirit continues to both teach and inspire us. The quiet fire of his generous spirit can continue to light us—down to the latest generation.

# Lincoln's Election Prayer

*"My Friends: No one, not in my situation, can appreciate my feeling of sadness at this parting. … Trusting in Him who can go with me, and remain with you, and be everywhere for good, let us confidently hope that all will yet be well."*

**-Abraham Lincoln**

http://bit.ly/2XCXvKF

**LINCOLN HAS JUST** won the election. He is now to be the president of the United States.

On the night of Nov. 6, when Lincoln first hears the results of his election at the telegraph office, he runs home, shouting, "Mary, we're elected!"

At this time, the United States is not very united at all. Southern states are declaring their independence from the country founded by the Declaration of Independence less than 100 years earlier. Lincoln has won the election by less than 40 percent of the votes.

On a rainy morning five days after the election, Lincoln boards a train with a yellow, red and gold-painted engine. He begins a tour of nearly 2,000 miles and seven states, bound for Washington, D.C. In an impromptu talk at the train station, with a thousand of his neighbors and townsfolk there to send him off, Lincoln begins his spiritual conversation with America—and with the world. It is a bittersweet conversation, with notes of both sadness and hope.

Lincoln's conversation that day is a spiritual one, because in it he defines God as a mystical presence—one that was there when George Washington became president and, likewise, is there with Lincoln. He believes that God, as a mystical presence, is there with the people who are waving good-bye—and He will continue to be there, with and between them, as the hundreds of miles and the days mount up.

Lincoln's train-station conversation begins spiritually, like a prayer. He is moved in his mind and heart to do something he almost always avoids doing—that is, speaking without notes. (Many of Lincoln's political speeches read like carefully constructed policy papers or poems.) As president-elect, he does not like to risk speaking without a manuscript.

This move is uniquely spontaneous. It is obvious that his heart is full. The moment is deep. It is a spiritual farewell address because of the depth of feeling, the profound definition of the history of the moment and because of the spiritual presence Lincoln calls forth. It is also a spiritual conversation because, at the very center of the situation of states leaving the Union, Lincoln sees most clearly not politics; not law; but a spiritual situation.

Lincoln always saw the unilateral breaking up of the states as a spiritual impossibility. What had brought the states together, into a nation, was a spiritual idea—human equality—and a spiritual bond of belief and sac-rifice. Something was created by the mutuality of the states that became greater than any one of them, and this could not be broken by any one of them without mutual consent by them all. The idea that a state could leave the Union was a legal fiction to him: it simply could not, in reality, be done. Like marriage itself, Lincoln believed that what God hath joined together no one could separate.

In this crisis, of course, there also were legal, moral, pragmatic and political reasons for the desire to separate, as well as economic and even geographical reasons. But Lincoln's belief in the country and the law had a spiritual, even mystical, root: The Union was sacred because God's pres-ence was not in the king, but in the people, and the people had made a nation.

This spiritual idea was not just pie in the sky; Lincoln describes it as coming from the very human depths of his life. To the gathering at the rail-way station he recites his personal history and his roots in the community.

"Here I have lived a quarter of a century… passed from being a young to an old man," Lincoln states. It is into this community that Lincoln's children were born, and here that one is buried. Lincoln's sense of God comes out of his personal and physical life, as well as the nation's history. The God who is with them, there, is a living God—one who aids people in doing His will and does not leave them. An abiding presence, "everywhere for good," is how Lincoln feels and knows God.

Lincoln concludes his train-station conversation with a benediction, a subtle statement of God's ongoing love. He says, "To His care commending you, as I hope in your prayers you will commend me, I bid you an affectionate farewell."

This is what a spiritual conversation sounds like, and it is in such an abiding presence—even in great difficulty, and after great elections—that we, too, can be commended, down to the latest generation.

# Spiritual Rivers

*"The Father of Waters again goes unvexed to the sea."*

**-Abraham Lincoln**

http://bit.ly/2JF2LU9

**THE QUOTE ABOVE** is so close to sounding like Shakespeare's iambic rhythms, yet these are words from Abraham Lincoln—the great admirer and reader of Shakespeare. Lincoln penned this line in a long letter he wrote to be read at a major political rally in Springfield, Illinois, late in the summer of 1863—the year of the Emancipation Proclamation, as well as of the Union victories in Gettysburg and Vicksburg that turned the tide of the Civil War.

*Unvexed.* Imagine a river being vexed and then unvexed. What poetry!

This is personification with depth. Lincoln portrays the great Mississippi River—just then liberated by General Grant at the city of Vicksburg—as a body of water that "wants" to flow freely. The river, in Lincoln's mind, is troubled and vexed, with its state of being in Southern slavery and racism. Like America and Americans, it wants to flow freely.

Both the river and the people have long been troubled—*vexed*—by slavery and by civil war. The river—all tied up in knots, confused and at cross purposes—is, in Lincoln's rhythmic quote, now open and free, as the country will be soon, as well. Unvexed. Without vexation.

This poetry about a river is key to Lincoln's spiritual life, too—and here's how:

All religions and spiritual practices see extraordinary natural places as meaningful. Rivers are one example: the Ganges River in India, and the

Jordan River in Israel. Certain desert spaces and mountains are seen as profound places as well—for example, Mount Sinai. Even the Buddha's Bodhi Tree is seen as sacred.

Rivers, along with the frontier prairie, figure into the development of Lincoln's life, mind and spirit. Twice, Lincoln takes flat boats down the great Mississippi River to New Orleans—like Huckleberry Finn! Lincoln also captains a steamboat—albeit unsuccessfully—down the Sangamon River, not unlike Mark Twain. The river was an escape from his father and a life of subsistence farming, and it is here that he earns his first real money—a silver half-dollar or two!—ferrying travelers from the shores of the Ohio River to mid-river steamboats.

In the classic movie *Young Mr. Lincoln*, we see the river portrayed three times. The director, John Ford, knew what he was doing. Film critic Geoffrey O'Brien wrote that, in the movie, Lincoln's "consciousness is the center of the movie and it remains as much a mystery as the river that is constantly evoked."

The river, in that great 1939 feature film, is the backdrop for Lincoln's love—and then loss—of Ann Rutledge: their courtship, and then her grave.

Later, it is the river that grabs Lincoln's attention when young Mary Todd is trying to flirt with him, at a ball, and it is the river that his traveling sidekick says is what is always on his mind. It's as if, his simple friend remarks, Lincoln is in love with the river like most men are in love with women!

In actuality, that statement is true! The spiritual power of Ford's focus on the river exemplifies it as a parable for Lincoln's reflections and his introspection. Looking at the river is Lincoln's way of pondering the distances of history and the world before him. Looking at the river is also how he moves closer to the inner recesses of his mind and heart.

In January of 1853, Lincoln went to a lecture by Ralph Waldo Emerson in Springfield, Illinois. He was, at this time, at a loss, unsure of what to do with his life and career. He heard Emerson state that "All life is a search for power"—and that all power is of one kind. "It is a sharing in the nature of the world," Emerson said.

To Lincoln, rivers defined the nature of the world—just like the unvexed Mississippi defined the freedom sought by Americans.

Emerson went on to say, in that 1853 lecture, that "the mind that is parallel with the laws of nature will be in the current of events, and strong with their strength."

The river of history was, to Lincoln, the real current. History was the event of those currents. His mind was aligned strongly with the strength of the laws of nature, two of which, of course, are freedom and equality.

So, might we, also, become unvexed and flow freely—with the strong current of history and the political mysticism of democracy. Like Lincoln, may we also be carried down in honor—to the latest generation.

# 4

# A Solemn Vow Before God

*"I made a solemn vow before God ..."*

-Abraham Lincoln

http://bit.ly/2jBfiiw

**THE QUOTE ABOVE** just about does it for the spiritual life of Abraham Lincoln, doesn't it?! There aren't too many mountain peaks higher than a solemn vow before God when you're quoting somebody's spiritual life.

But the word "God" is like an on/off switch as Americans hear it today. Millions of us say, "Ah, yes." Millions more say, "Oh, no." And some say, "What?!"

Perhaps more polarizing is that in politics, the word "God" is a great divider. God either means everything to the believer or nothing to the nonbeliever. It is, in our time, an increasingly antique word—one with meanings that, in some cases, summon images of old tag sales and flea markets of the last century. Personally, I regret this being the case.

But what could Lincoln have meant, making a vow before God—and what could that mean for us today? Well, let's climb this God-mountain. Let's try to reach that peak where we might see what Lincoln saw about God.

We do know that Lincoln did not refer to any one particular church's God. Like many today, Lincoln felt that church creeds fail to include the universal, even democratic, nature of God.

Lincoln was born on the same day and in the same year as Charles Darwin: Feb. 12, 1809. Both Lincoln and Darwin reached a zenith of influence in their adult years, at a time when science, biology and the theory of evolution were secularizing the biblical view of creation. Supposedly, General Pickett stated, at Gettysburg, that he could not believe that Robert E. Lee was descended from apes—and certainly Lincoln would not have called us to follow the better "apes of our nature." No, Lincoln kept his eye on our better "angels" at a time when the image of God in human life was losing its traditional, sacred meaning.

Lincoln also was familiar with the economic theories of Karl Marx, as was his law partner. Economic and material determinism was vying for the vow of humanity around the world as Lincoln's century progressed.

How did Lincoln see the almighty dollar when he made a vow before God pertaining to the property called "slaves"? Property is, after all, central to the Constitution.

While we are trying to climb this God-mountain, we can note that by the time most of Lincoln's historical interpreters came along, Freud's ideas were also in the cultural mix—and interpreters noted that those references to God just might be a sign of Lincoln's father complex.

It turns out that looking for God at the top of a mountain is not what Lincoln had meant at all; in making his vow before God, Lincoln was, instead, saying something about himself. Lincoln was not saying something about God, but rather was reflecting on something deep within himself. It was from within the valley of the shadow of the world and its sorrows that Lincoln spoke. I'll quote from a recent novel that gives us a view into Lincoln's mind and heart: George Saunders' *Lincoln in the Bardo*:

> [Lincoln's] ... mind was freshly inclined toward sorrow; toward the fact that the world was full of sorrow ... therefore one must do what one could to lighten the load of those with whom one came into contact ... given that his position in the world situated him to be either of great help or great harm, it would not do to stay low, if he could help it. (p. 304)

Sorrow was a political category to Lincoln. The Godly response—the ethical and spiritual response—was to help. That response was what a vow before God sealed for Lincoln. It was universal human sympathy that called him to act, and for him the providence of God was the canopy over humanity. Slavery was the most sorrowful and the most unjust reality of his time, and so to begin the emancipation of the sorrowful burden that white people inflicted on black people was a solemn responsibility to him—"under God," as he would say in the Gettysburg Address.

Lincoln's Cabinet was astounded that this president saw God acting in history and saw himself acting in light of God's will. In such charity and justice, we, too, can act in honor—down to the latest generation.

# 5

# Way Over Yonder

*"As to his religious nature, it seems to me to have certainly
been of the amplest, deepest-rooted, loftiest kind."*

-Walt Whitman, describing Abraham Lincoln

http://bit.ly/2jCWRtN

WALT WHITMAN WAS a careful observer of Abraham Lincoln. He
would often watch as Lincoln and his military escorts rode past him on
Vermont Avenue on summer mornings, on their way to the White House.

Whitman wrote, about those momentary encounters:

"I see very plainly Abraham Lincoln's dark brown face, with deep-cut
lines; the eyes, always to me with a deep latent sadness in the expression.
We have got so that we exchange bows, and very cordial ones."

Whitman also saw in Lincoln's face what he called an "indirect expression." He would comment that, "There is something else there."

Another poet, Carl Sandburg, had a name for that "something else" in
Lincoln's face. Sandberg described it with the word "yonder."

*Yonder* was one of Sandberg's favorite words. The term shows up in
many of his *Rootabaga* stories. Sandburg imagines that Lincoln got his
sense of yonder from his mother. "Nancy Hanks," wrote Sandburg,
"believed in God, in the Bible, in mankind, in the past and future, in babies,
people, animals, flowers, fishes, in foundations and roofs—in time and in
the eternities outside of time ..." He concludes his lexicon of her beliefs
by stating that "so much of what she believed was yonder—always yonder."

These two poets, as they thought about Lincoln, saw something spiritual about him: a religious nature, a deep sorrow, a sense of yonder.

You might ponder the benefit of a president with a sad and "yonder" spirit. You might also wonder how Lincoln got so much done, as president, if he was so spiritual. Good questions like these can lead to great insights.

It is a third poet, the Indian mystic Rabindranath Tagore, who can tell us of the usefulness of a sense of yonder in a person's life. Tagore writes of the mystic vision that the ancient Indian holy men had derived from the way they saw the vast lands and thick forests around them. India, then, was similar to the Indiana that young Lincoln had experienced when he lived there, having arrived in 1816: vast lands and thick, primeval forests.

The wisdom of the ancient sages was simple: The aim of life is not to acquire, but to realize. Their response to the natural world was to enlarge the consciousness; to grow into one's surroundings. The natural world and the world of humankind are one, according to these sages. Together, these worlds create a great truth, a harmony.

To the primitive natural world Lincoln grew up in, his response was in the same spirit—a spirit that he never lost. He did not hunt or fish, and he only shot one animal—a turkey. Nine-year-old Lincoln even cried at the turkey's beauty when he approached it. He chastised his friends when they put hot coals on the backs of turtles. His natural instinct—his spiritual reflex—was to see himself as one with nature: to envision a harmony with life, not a conquest. Sorrow and sadness came naturally to Lincoln, too, with his mother and sister both dying before he was 20 years old.

The vast size of frontier America and the prairies of Illinois communicated, to Lincoln, unity and wonder.

Lincoln's sense of yonder was a kind of hope that came from how he saw his place in nature. People on the East Coast initially thought that he was uncouth, when in actuality, he was ragged and rugged—a bit like a traditional Indian holy man.

But Lincoln was not *just* like an Indian mystic. He believed in history as well as nature, and he believed in American civilization. America was to be a unified country, Lincoln believed; the land, as well as the Constitution, told him so.

Abraham Lincoln was a spiritual man, and his spirit continues to teach and inspire us. In yonder and in sorrow, his spirit can continue to light us—down to the latest generation.

# 6

# Finding the Right Word

*"Mr. Lincoln, what are you doing?"*

**-Billy Herndon, to Abraham Lincoln**

http://bit.ly/2jBfiPy

**LINCOLN'S LAW PARTNER,** the young Billy Herndon, always called him "Mr. Lincoln." And so, on the day Herndon asked him what he was doing, what *was* Mr. Lincoln doing? Why, he was sitting on their office floor. He was hugging his knees—and apparently, when Herndon discovered him, he had been curled up in a ball like that for quite a while. Lincoln's reply? "I'm looking for the right word." The "right word" meant everything to Abraham Lincoln. His spiritual life is most clearly visible to us through his words.

Lincoln's language—his word choice—shows us quite distinctly his ideas, his values and the terrain of his spirit. Like old stone walls in New England, Lincoln lines up his words to outline his thought. His words take into account the lay of the land and his phrases speak to the facts on the ground: our history.

When he says, at the end of the Gettysburg Address, "of the people, by the people, for the people" he is, of course, standing before—almost amongst—a crowded field of standing people. There are upward of 20,000 people present.

When, at the end of his second Inaugural Address, he speaks of caring "for him who shall have borne the battle and for his widow, and his orphan," the crowd is filled with men who have missing arms or legs. The war-wounded survivors are everywhere, and Lincoln chose words that spoke to them, even *for* them.

So, here's a word Lincoln picked that stands out (like Shakespeare, he sometimes practically invented a word, although this one was used by Milton in the 17th century): "disenthrall."

We don't expect a presidential speech to focus on our state of being "enthralled" or "disenthralled." Maybe a novelist or a poet would write about such a word concept, but this was Lincoln telling Congress that they must "disenthrall." By this, Lincoln meant that they (and we) must wake up to what is really going on. We must put away our old ways of thinking and seeing, putting away what he called "the dogmas of the quiet past."

This was Lincoln's call—a very *American* call—to spiritual renewal: to think anew, to act anew. It is only after this renewal that Lincoln believes we can save our country. Salvation comes from renewal, and one historian says that Lincoln was "crafting an alternative vision of reality."

Spiritual transformation and spiritual change is, of course, the work of religion. But Lincoln also makes it the work of *all the people*. He makes it a political thing to do, as well.

Lincoln, more than any other president and most writers, brings together two parts of our lives: the spiritual and the political, the sacred and the secular. Furthermore, he does it without mixing church and state. His clear words encompass the real fields of life and give us a spirit for life. Through Lincoln, we find spirit in words and phrases like "charity," "new birth of freedom" and "the mystic chords of memory."

Abraham Lincoln was a spiritual man, and his spirit continues to teach us—through his very particular words—down to the latest generation.

# 7

# Solace in 'the Fiery Trial'

*"We must disenthrall ourselves. ... The fiery trial through which we pass, will light us down, in honor or dishonor, to the latest generation. "*

**-Abraham Lincoln**

http://bit.ly/2jBfjmA

**LINCOLN WROTE THE** words above to Congress in a very dark time, in 1862. Lincoln's party had just suffered significant defeats in the midterm elections, and Lincoln's new Union Army was suffering more defeats than victories as the war increased.

This, then, was Lincoln's pivotal moment. Lincoln had long been enthralled with the value of America's past: the Constitution and Jefferson, the Revolution and Washington. Now he was saying that Americans must "disenthrall" themselves, and that only then, the country could be saved. With the present so bleak and the past too dim, Lincoln proposes a leap of faith, an alternative future. In a long speech, Lincoln proposes Constitutional amendments to rid the country of slavery. Lincoln suggests buying back the slaves (though at great cost), or easing out slavery by the year 1900—35 years into the future.

"Disenthrall" is one of Lincoln's most exact, and most inventive, verbs. Holding fast to that which is good will not be enough. Americans—united—must let go as they travel forward, into the future. Historian Ron White defines what Lincoln is doing as "crafting an alternative vision of reality ... to move beyond ... limited worldviews and embrace a future that could not be fully known."

In the spiritual life of Lincoln, this is the working of his "yonder" vision. This is his capacity to endure uncertainty, to tolerate ambiguity. This is his Zen-poise moment.

How did Lincoln come to stand on the deck of a storm-tossed ship and see light on the darkening horizon?

One legacy for Lincoln's strength of vision is one not often noted: the women who knew and loved him.

When his calm and even mystical mother, Nancy Hanks, died when he was only 9 years old, her words to him and his sister were to be good and to love their father. Her focus was on virtue and the future—not the past, the hardships and the loss. This woman's spirit was formed by her biblical religion. In a song that Lincoln heard her sing, it is recited:

> You may bury me in the east,
>
> You may bury me in the west,
>
> And we'll all rise together in that morning.

"Rising together" is what President Lincoln was calling on both Congress and the nation to do—this is his alternative future, in which all rise together to a new day. He even says that "… we must rise with the occasion …"

Now, rising "with" an occasion is not the same as rising "to" an occasion—the former is a matter of all being together, "we." Amid rising waters, Lincoln believed community to be as vital as courage.

Lincoln always referred to his inspirational birth mother as "my sweet angel mother," to distinguish her from his equally loved and inspirational stepmother, Sarah Bush.

But if his "rise-up" spirit came from his birth mother, a certain "light-down" spirit came to him later, from a female minister in a prayer meeting at the White House. Noted Quaker minister Eliza P. Gurney, along with three other women, had come to see Lincoln for the sole purpose of giving him spiritual comfort in his heavy presidential burdens. Gurney preached an encouraging sermon and then got down on her knees before Lincoln, praying for heavenly light for him.

Afterward, Lincoln wrote Gurney a personal and religious letter saying that, indeed, it was a fiery trial through which they were passing. Quoted from the New Testament, 1 Peter 4:12: "Beloved, do not be surprised at the fiery trial that is taking place among you to test you, as though something strange were happening to you."

In dark times, Lincoln was asked by his mother to rise up, with his sister, and to be good. And in dark times with the nation, Lincoln called on Congress to rise up and to be honorable. He called on Congress and the people, in their fiery trial, to rise up together: to see a future, and to be lighted down in honor—to the latest generation.

# 8

# Hating More—or Loving More

*"He must always make enemies, for then he can be sure he exists."*

**-Poet W. H. Auden, on the leading character of Shakespeare's *Richard III***

http://bit.ly/2jCWSxR

**ALWAYS MAKING ENEMIES** is, of course, opposite of the nature of Abraham Lincoln. Yet this act defines the main character in one of Lincoln's favorite Shakespearean plays.

In *Richard III*, the "bad" king, Richard, has to make enemies just so he knows he's alive, writes W.H. Auden.

Richard's opening line, "Now is the winter of our discontent ..." describes something that was supposedly made glorious by the new sunshine of his brother becoming king, thereby settling the terrible civil wars that had plagued England for 30 years—what we call the War of the Roses. But Richard is not happy that their civil war could be over, because he has ambition to be king. Making enemies along the way is self-assuring to him.

Lincoln knew what we all learn as the play goes on: that "now," in fact, the winter will continue. The bad king is so ambitious that he will lie and do anything necessary to get what he wants—including turning against those closest to him.

Lincoln would have first read these lines and this play in his school readers, perhaps even as a youngster. The theme of ambition corrupting honor was a lesson he took to heart. Throughout his life, Lincoln never let his ambition corrupt his honor. Unlike the bad king, who hates more in order to know that he exists, Lincoln actually loved more—and then he loved some more.

Some critics say that Americans can't really accept a dark view. They attest that Americans view tragedy and evil as "un-American." Instead, we hope to overcome tragedy and evil, much like the sunshine will make winter's discontent turn into glorious summer.

Optimism.

Yet others say that Lincoln himself was both deeper and ahead of his time in how he could see the bitterness and irony in King Richard. Lincoln could see it for what it was—blind self-destruction—without becoming what it was—self-destructive.

We can imagine Lincoln being able to understand, even then, what English poet Auden would write many years later about King Richard: that he had to make everyone into an enemy just to feel alive, just to know that he existed.

This clear-eyed aspect of Lincoln's character shows up in his view of how misguided the South had become. Lincoln never hated the South; on the contrary, he had deep Southern roots. Lincoln's wife's sister, as well as some cousins, were Confederates. While addressing Northerners, Lincoln once said that "we" would think and act "like them" if in their social situation. He knew that it was hard to rise above tribe and clan and social pressure, even though he did that himself.

Lincoln said that the South had been telling itself "sugar-coated" stories—even lies—for decades. Southerners had been told things like "slavery is good," and that black men and women were "happy." They were even told that armed rebellion could work. All of that turned out to be what Lincoln always knew it was: sugar-coating. In other words, sweetened lies.

Lincoln could see evil darkness for what it was—blind ambition—and he could see sugar-coated propaganda for what it was—fake news.

The winter of discontent really did come to the South after the war. If winter means that one's way of life is darkened and even destroyed, then that is what happened to Southerners. The slave-driven way of life was over, and a new society had to be constructed in its place. But race-hatred didn't go away, and after the Civil War, the South simply rebuilt the segregated society it'd had before—but this time, without outright slavery. That society, albeit somewhat reformed, had to be torn down again in the midst of the Civil Rights movement. Even now, the social poison of racism has not been fully healed.

But what did Lincoln offer the South, whom he did not hate? What did Lincoln offer in place of angry resentment? He offered the idea of a future America: a house where freedom was tempered by equality and equality was made joyful by freedom.

For the South, then—like any society that is on the edge of collapse—all ideas of ethical goodness had to change. Behaviors toward one other had to change. In a time of cultural devastation, the role of ethics and the idea of hope became crucial.

Author and scholar Jonathan Lear published a book called *Radical Hope: Ethics in the Face of Cultural Devastation*. This title describes the challenge that Lincoln faced: how to find hope—radical hope—in a time of cultural devastation.

In the Gettysburg Address, Lincoln's offer of hope was a new birth of freedom. That newfound hope was not just for the North; it was for America. For Lincoln, the "new" America also included the South. A new birth of freedom was a part of the ending of the winter of discontent.

Lincoln knew that he existed because, unlike the "bad" king who could not be a lover and so became a willful villain, he had—and we have—better angels in our nature.

And so, in the hope of the coming summer sunlight, we, too, can be lighted down in honor—even to the latest generation.

# 9

# A Hair from the Head of Lincoln

*"Please wear it tomorrow; you are one of the men who most thoroughly understands and appreciates Lincoln."*

**-John Hay, in a note to President Theodore Roosevelt**

http://bit.ly/2jBfjTC

**IN THE QUOTE** above, what is John Hay asking Theodore Roosevelt to do? He is asking him to wear a gift: a gold ring that holds, under its clear stone, a beautifully encircled hair from the head of Abraham Lincoln.

John Hay had been Roosevelt's Secretary of State for three years, and "tomorrow," Roosevelt was going to be inaugurated president for his second term. Roosevelt was deeply moved. He wore the ring.

This is a tidbit of information from the secular history of America, but what it has to do with the spiritual life of Lincoln is this: Lincoln's life reveals its meaning through spiritual—and even, at times, religious—terms.

The gold ring gifted by Hay is a relic, with its physical remnant of Lincoln. It was 19th-century custom, after all: locks of hair were exchanged and framed in pictures and art objects throughout late Victorian culture. That secular custom may seem foreign to us today, though.

The history of religion is a chronicle of relics handed down, touched and even worshiped by and through generations. Though called superstitious by some, relics carry in matter the meaning of sacred ideas. Relics are found inside Buddhist statues and in Christian chapels. Sacred objects are found in all religions, and of course, we personally treasure objects from our own past and family. So, a relic of Lincoln is another illustration of the way his secular life takes on a spiritual dimension.

A relic of Lincoln would have meant a great deal to Teddy Roosevelt. There is a photograph of Lincoln's funeral procession, winding through the streets of New York City, in which historians have been able to accurately identify a young boy in a white shirt leaning out the upper-story window of a New York home: It is the 6-year-old Teddy Roosevelt. Lincoln's funeral procession deeply affected him.

In his adult life, Teddy Roosevelt had an inkwell on his desk in Sagamore Hill that bore a small bust of Lincoln. But it was the living spirit of Lincoln that Roosevelt treasured more.

In one of his most important and formative speeches, Roosevelt cites what he calls the "high purposes of Abraham Lincoln" as being the guiding light for the dark and terrible times through which he, Roosevelt, and his generation were passing. In Roosevelt's time, America was maneuvering the huge conflict between corporations and labor, between the very few of the Gilded Age and the laboring, suffering masses.

Roosevelt felt there was a thread running through American history—from Washington, to Lincoln, to himself—that had meaning for the nation and for all of humankind. That thread was, according to Roosevelt, the value of a government created to help ensure the fairness and equality of life.

In preparation for one notable speech, Roosevelt chose another religious tradition: that of honoring sacred sites, places made meaningful usually by sacrifice or bloodshed. Religions mark such sacred sites, and people return to them for inspiration. Such a place for America and Roosevelt was a little town in Kansas called Osawatomie. For in this town, the first blood of the American war against slavery had been shed; it was there that John Brown defended his town against the armed, pro-slavery men. It was there that John Brown's son was killed. So, in 1910, Roosevelt went to this site in what had been called Bleeding Kansas and spoke to crowds of people about the Civil War and about the coming battle between the rich and the poor. Roosevelt saw democratic hope embodied in the old men standing before his train platform.

And, like anyone at a sacred site, Roosevelt declared, "I care for the great deeds of the past …" He cared because such deeds can, he believed, lead others to see truth and virtue.

During that speech, Roosevelt went on to say, about the corporations: "It is necessary that laws should be passed to prohibit the use of corporate funds directly or indirectly for political purposes."

President Barack Obama returned to Osawatomie in his first term, to speak of Teddy Roosevelt's "new" nationalism—a nationalism that supported a strong government to keep the rich from getting richer at the price of destroying the equality so central to fairness and freedom.

Such are the mystic chords of memory, the relics and the sites—like a gold ring and a small town in Kansas—that can light us down in honor, to the latest generation.

# God's 'Almost Chosen People'

*"I shall be most happy indeed if I shall be a humble instrument in the hands of the Almighty, and of this His almost chosen people."*

**-Abraham Lincoln, 1861**

http://bit.ly/2jCWT4T

**WHAT DID ABRAHAM** Lincoln mean by his mysterious phrase about God's "almost chosen people"? After all, there were a lot of people rooting for Lincoln's presidency who were sure that they were more than "almost" chosen. Like many people both then and now, the idea of being "God's people" and "on God's side" is, by thought, what a nation is all about. But Lincoln was not one of them. Folks in the so-called American Party, or Know-Nothing Party, were afraid that Catholics and Irish immigrants would destroy American society. For Lincoln, the principle of equality was basic to the idea of America. Without it, he said, he would rather move to Czarist Russia, where they take their despotism straight and without hypocrisy. To him, it was hypocrites—not Catholics—who could destroy American society.

People who tried to pick out the "right" Americans in the flood of immigrants were, to Lincoln, wrong-headed. In 1855, Lincoln wrote to his best friend, stating that when you say that the idea of equality applies to you but not to them, you are on the road to degeneracy. For Lincoln, the oppression of the black people was where such degeneracy began.

Here is why Lincoln's idea of America has something to do with his spiritual life: If America was comprised only of God's "almost chosen people," then who were *we* to begin totally closing and rejecting "real" Americans? Who were *we* to create an elite elect?

Lincoln was a deep reader of the Bible. He would have noted that the bands of brothers in the Bible all have a role to play in God's story. For example, Isaac and Ishmael both had Abraham as their father. In Genesis, he says he will be with both. God may choose, but God does not reject. Rabbi Jonathan Sacks recently wrote, on a similar plane of thought, that when Abraham dies, half-brothers Isaac and Ishmael stand together peacefully at his grave. Islam is God's presence through Ishmael.

Politically, Lincoln chose the North, but he never rejected the South. To him, the North and the South were always brothers, not enemies. What he rejected was unlawful rebellion and slavery—and about that, he would fight.

But remember, Lincoln said that he would be "most happy indeed" if he could be "a humble instrument" of both God and the American people. At the end of the war, that humility shows. He wanted to win the war, but he didn't want to reject the brothers who lost. That's because he was a spiritual man, believing, as the Psalms say, that God's "tender mercies are over all his works" (Psalm 145:9)—even down to the latest generation.

# The Spiral Pattern of Generations

http://bit.ly/2jCWU8X

**IN PLACE OF** a quote at the start of this chapter, let us pause for a moment to consider Feb. 12, 1809—Lincoln's birthday.

Lincoln was born into a remarkable generation of idealists. He was certainly one of the poorest, too, living a primitive life for his first years.

I wonder what he thought when reading Jesus's Sermon on the Mount: "Blessed are you who are poor, for yours is the kingdom of God." From Lincoln's low estate, he not only lifted himself; he lifted his country.

There were many idealists in Lincoln's generation: consider the New England transcendentalist Ralph Waldo Emerson, or the brave slave revolutionary Nat Turner, or the women's suffrage activist Susan B. Anthony. Even Queen Victoria was an idealist. When each of these individuals came of age, their high values led to high dramas and high consequences.

Lincoln was born four generations after George Washington and came to power four generations after the American Revolution. When Washington was called "The Father of His Country," many, many young people followed him and regarded him as their leader. When Lincoln was an older man, he was called "Father Abraham," and many, many young people followed him into the Civil War.

Four generations after Lincoln was born, Franklin D. Roosevelt was born; four generations after the Civil War, Roosevelt was an elder leader—and many, many young people followed him into World War II.

If there are turning wheels to history, generation to generation, then those called Baby Boomers—who were born four generations after Franklin Roosevelt—are the elder leaders now, as we enter this new dark time.

Are the young people now, born four generations after the Boomers, the heroes who will follow the idealists of the New Age into the coming struggle? From the looks of climate-change fighters and the #MeToo and Time's Up activists, they are.

Can aging Baby Boomers be the inspirational idealists now, as elders, to a young generation of enthusiastic followers? Will these old and young people turn the tide of American history once again?

Are there elders now who, like Lincoln, are able to guide and lead highly idealistic young people who are full of transcendental ideas and ideals? So many people say, these days: "Where is our Lincoln now?" That is why the spiritual life of Lincoln is so important.

When Lincoln became president the mainline churches fell apart, splitting into Northern and Southern fragments. Newspapers polarized into political weapons; the power of vested financial interests ruled politicians; technological changes began to pull apart the fabric of town and family. The institutions of society could no longer hold the center. Political principles were broken. Lincoln was elected because there were at least four new political parties and the older ones were dividing.

This is when Lincoln said, "The fiery trial through which we pass will light us down in honor or dishonor to the latest generation."

He also stated that, "The dogmas of the quiet past are inadequate to the stormy present. The occasion is piled high with difficulty and we must rise—with the occasion. As our case is new so we much think anew and act anew. We must disenthrall ourselves, and then we shall save our country."

Lincoln began the words above, in his speech, with a simple phrase: "Fellow citizens, we cannot escape history."

And so we are looking at a spiral pattern of history in which the spiritual life of Lincoln suddenly looks like the mast, or the rudder, for our foundering ship.

We know that there were legions of young people who were not cynical about America at Lincoln's time; they wanted to save what they saw as American civilization and the democratic hope for the world. There were bands of young who called themselves the Wide Awakes. They paraded and campaigned for Lincoln, and they sang of Lincoln—and of liberty, too. They ordered themselves into scout-like troops and got uniforms and even minor firearms. They prepared themselves for what history was preparing for them. It was national service in a conflict for the survival of the world as they knew it.

We know that the young Teddy Roosevelt felt the fire of this time. The idealism of Lincoln rose in Roosevelt's own generation, expanding to take up the fight for the survival of democracy and equality against the corporations and the trusts. The idealists of Roosevelt's generation wanted to break the hold of Wall Street on the labor movement; to substantially aide in the progress of race relations; and to conserve our great natural resources. All of this occurred, in Roosevelt's mind, in the spirit of Abraham Lincoln.

It just may be that, more than two centuries after the birth of Lincoln, new generations of people are ready to follow an aged, transcendental idealist like Lincoln once again—in order to find a new birth of freedom and a world "of the people, by the people, for the people." This spirit can make the young wide awake and relight the fire inside the old, leading us down in honor—to the latest generation.

# 12

# When Death Still Shocked Us

*"Oft as the rolling years bring back this hour, let it again, however briefly, be dwelt upon. For my own part I hope and intend till my own dying day, whenever the fourteenth or fifteenth of April comes, to annually gather a few friends and hold its tragic reminiscence."*

**-Walt Whitman, following the death of Abraham Lincoln**

http://bit.ly/2jCWUFZ

**LINCOLN WAS SHOT** on the evening of April 14, 1865, and died the next morning, on April 15. Walt Whitman marked those two dates with annual talks on the meaning of Lincoln's death—not only on the meaning of his life, but also on the meaning of his death.

Whitman saw Lincoln's death as a unifying moment in American history; as the first great unifying moment in the drama of our country. He called Lincoln our "first great Martyr Chief." He capitalized both *Martyr* and *Chief*. Here, Whitman is thinking about the written tragedies of Shakespeare and the Greeks. He sees that, in the story of a people, the people become one when they share in a great grief. On Lincoln, Whitman says, "He was assassinated—but the Union is not assassinated."

It would be hard to measure the shock to the new nation, divided as it was, when the news of Lincoln's death came.

Here is part of my own poem about this shock:

> When you lay still those long nine hours, your last night—a small, narrow room at the end of the first floor; a tailor's house, the bed too small, your knees bent—and as your personal silence began a great gasp, a roar of dumb grief began to cross the land in torrents.

As errant blood soaked up the Burns, the Byron, and the Shakespeare that had been your daily food and drink, another great cry and stun, at the final news, tore across the land.

In America today we have witnessed too many prominent assassinations. Millions still remember John F. Kennedy's murder, followed by the killing of his brother, Bobby; Martin Luther King, Jr.; and Malcolm X.

We are no longer shockable, it would seem.

In the spiritual life of Lincoln, thinking about death is an essential aspect of the journey. Lincoln thought about death all his life. To think about the death of Lincoln is, spiritually, to begin to realize that America can break your heart.

Here is a moment in time when Lincoln was thinking about death:

It was Sunday—Palm Sunday—and April 9, 1865. Lincoln was steaming up the Potomac River from Richmond to Washington aboard the River Queen. Unknowingly, he was entering his last week of life—at least, in the way we usually credit how we know things.

What was on Lincoln's mind that day?

He had visited the destroyed and vacant Confederate capitol, refusing a hosanna-style parade or a "mission accomplished" boast. He was ingloriously rowed ashore and then he walked the streets, telling kneeling blacks that only God should be knelt to. A rifle was seen pointing at Lincoln out of an upstairs window. A Connecticut soldier said that they were greeted as Roman conquerors—only, Lincoln would have none of that.

On his voyage back, Lincoln read Shakespeare aloud to his traveling party. His French companion, Marquis de Chambrun, wrote this later: "I cannot recall this reading without being awed at the remembrance ..."

Lincoln was reading from *Macbeth*, which was among his favorite plays. He read the passage containing Macbeth's offence and guilt for killing the king.

"Offense" was a word Lincoln had known all his life, starting with the readers he studied during his brief time in a classroom as a boy. *Offense* was a big idea for youths in those days, and young people were expected to learn from the heavily religious and morally freighted books. Lincoln was a boy with a heavy conscience.

Was Lincoln somehow feeling guilty at this time, on his return trip from the Confederate capital? He was the victorious king, after all. Was Lincoln somehow feeling aware of his death? Soon, his assassination would be the first American regicide.

Lincoln's French companion went on to write about Lincoln's focus on the horrible torments of Macbeth's mind, describing, "… [he] was struck by the weird beauty of these verses, or by a vague presentiment coming over him … "

Ambition had always been a real conflict, a deep ambiguity, to Lincoln. What would fame ever gain a person, he would say, when time itself was an empty vapor?

He went on to explain at great length, to his rapt passengers, just how true the passages on Macbeth's guilt really were. How did Lincoln know about such guilt? Well, he had just sat in the chair of traitor Jefferson Davis. He had overseen and pursued war. But Lincoln had never personally killed a man. Even as a boy, he had only slain one bird—a turkey—and he was very sorry he had.

So, Lincoln is reading about the death of a king. Often, he searched Shakespeare or the Bible for hope that his recently deceased son, Willie, was somehow in eternity or with God.

When Lincoln left Springfield for the White House, his stepmother had worried, feeling sure that "something" would happen to him. His partner said that Lincoln had felt the same. In his farewell speech, then, he offered the sentiment that he did not know if he would ever return. He did have dreams of some foreboding quality, often of a ship rushing to shore.

On his last day, on a carriage ride with Mary, he spoke of visiting the Holy Lands—and, there, seeing the places of even greater kings than he: David and Solomon.

You have to wonder: What memory and desire were mixing for him, in this cruel month? What was the state of Lincoln's spirit?

As memories and desire mix, and feeling America's story now, as we do, perhaps Lincoln's brooding, meditative spirit can guide us down in honor—even to the latest generation.

# 13

# Horse-sense

*"I should say the invisible foundations and vertebra of his character,
more than any man's in history, were mystical, abstract, moral
and spiritual—while upon all of them was built, and out of all
of them radiated ... what the vulgar call horse-sense."*

**-Walt Whitman, in *Memories of President Lincoln***

http://bit.ly/2jCWVd1

**LINCOLN, WHITMAN SAYS,** had a mystical and spiritual foundation to his character. But here's the odd thing: as mystical and spiritual as those pillars were in Lincoln, he was completely controlled—grounded, we could say—by what common people call "horse-sense." So, Lincoln may have had his head in heavenly clouds, but his feet were firmly on the earthly ground.

We can see this twofold nature when we study Lincoln's face, and especially his eyes. He had vision—yonder-sight. He also had vigilance—hawk-eyed, razor-sharp perception.

*Horse-sense* is a funny term, though. What does it mean?

It turns out (after consulting dictionary references to the phrase) that it's not a bad quality for a President to have. It means having good judgement, avoiding trouble, not making rash mistakes.

Therefore, Walt Whitman is giving Lincoln a double compliment here. He is saying that Lincoln is spiritual in his vision and yet practical in his action.

What is important about this combination in the spiritual life of Lincoln is that it is the very same dual aspect that classic Christian saints possess. Most saints, it turns out, don't just have their heads in the clouds, close to God; no, they have their legs and feet on the ground, with the common people. Whichever saint or saintly person you can think of, he or she will likely have this combination of high mindedness and common touch. Certainly the present Dalai Lama is a brilliant scholar of ancient Buddhists texts, and yet he has an almost childlike, common way of talking and being with people. The Buddha, too. Joan of Arc. Jesus.

Seeing Lincoln with a personal characteristic like a saint goes to show that his spiritual life was not a frill or fluke, it was the adamant core of who he was. Lincoln's combination of the spiritual and the ordinary places him in a long lineage of spiritual traditions.

Lincoln, as a calm and prudent president, is still politically relevant to us today. Lincoln, as a saint with "horse-sense," is relevant to us spiritually, as well.

Saint Thomas Aquinas was another man of "horse-sense." I don't imagine that Lincoln knew much about the 13th-century Saint Thomas Aquinas—perhaps the most brilliant theologian in history. But Lincoln would have liked him. Aquinas was called "the dumb ox" because he was a heavy, wine-barrel of a man who was strong as an ox; he was also very, very silent, so people mistook him for being dumb. He would have reminded Lincoln of his ox-like father, who also was named Thomas—except that Aquinas was kind. Silence was deep in the character of Lincoln, as well.

Saint Thomas Aquinas and Abraham Lincoln would have been soul brothers if they had known each other. Not just for "horse-sense," either. Both revered reason and the human capacity for reason. Aquinas brought science into the Middle Ages by his reverence for reason. He thought that reason is as essential to the mind and body of a person as God is to life. Reason is, he believed, our inner God. Lincoln's first real faith was in reason, and he taught himself logic. He gave speeches as a young politician and lawyer on how reason would save our nation; how it could serve as a civil religion.

It was not a highfalutin version of reason that Lincoln stood by, either. This was reason that led to common-sense ideas, to "horse-sense" decisions. The same was said of Aquinas, by English writer G.K. Chesterton: "The fact that Thomism is the philosophy of common sense is itself a matter of common sense."

Neither Lincoln nor Aquinas was wildly emotional in his spiritual life, and each rooted himself in the common sense of ordinary people.

"[Aquinas had] a conception of brotherhood broader than most modern democracy," wrote Chesterton.

What unites these two saints, one primarily religious and the other mainly secular? Common, ordinary people, the life of reason, faith and "horse-sense." Such is the spirit we see in Lincoln. We, too, can join in having reason guide us, as it guided him—down to the latest generation.

# 14

# Lincoln's Physical Strength

*"I'm the big buck of this lick!"*

**-Abraham Lincoln**

http://bit.ly/2jCWWh5

**WHO SAID THE** quote above? It was Abe Lincoln, as a young man! And who did he say it to? He most likely said it to Jack Armstrong, leader of the Clary's Grove boys. And why did he say it? Was he picking a fight? No.

Lincoln didn't pick fights, but fights—like war itself—came to him because he was so strong. Strong young men in 1830s Illinois challenged each other to fight all the time—to see who was the strongest, for the fun of a good race, for a wrestle or for a clobbering. Jack Armstrong himself used to wrestle people and then put them in a barrel and roll them down a hill! As the new man in town (New Salem, Illinois, 1830), Lincoln was 6 feet, 4 inches tall and weighed a hard-as-nails 180 pounds. He often faced challengers.

When you study Lincoln's life, words and thoughts, you also feel his physical presence. Lincoln was not a "talking head." In fact, his body itself continues to interest people. There are three recently published books that focus on how his body, even in death, is a relic—a monument of meaning to Americans. But it is his *living* body that started giving life to his spirit.

These days, thanks to yoga and meditation, acupuncture and healing, we talk about embodied spirituality. Yet the triangle of body, mind and spirit is ancient. In the spiritual life of Abraham Lincoln, we know that his mind and spirit were astonishing—but so was his body.

Here's one quick story about Lincoln's strength: One day, while out reviewing the troops during the Civil War, Lincoln was asked if he was tired. He said, "Why, no!" and took up an axe and chopped some firewood just to show how strong and able and well he was.

Then he took the axe and held it out straight from his shoulder—and just kept holding it out there, as a demonstration of his physical power. When he left, several of the young soldiers tried to do it themselves—and they could not! They must have been amazed that this ancient-looking, gangly president was so strong!

Think it's easy? Try it yourself.

On his deathbed, when Lincoln was taken out of his clothes and changed into a nightshirt, the gathered men were astonished at how powerful Lincoln's long, bare arms looked.

"The better to hold the country together with," Lincoln might have cracked.

Abraham Lincoln was a spiritual man, and his spirit continues to teach and inspire us. Even in his physical strength, he can move us to strength and purpose—down to the latest generation.

# 15

# A Sacred Effort

*"... those divine attributes which the believers in a
living God always ascribe to Him ..."*

http://bit.ly/2jBfkXG

**THE QUOTE ABOVE** is part of an important sentence in Lincoln's
second Inaugural Address, which discusses the cause of the Civil War and
the lengthy suffering it induced. The "divine attribute" that Lincoln has in
mind here is a passage from the Bible, from Psalms 19:9—that "the judg-
ments of the Lord are true and righteous altogether."

Why is Lincoln talking in this way? His second Inaugural Address
is famous for its brevity. So why did he devote an extended passage to a
major theological interpretation of history?

He wasn't doing this as politicians might today—to win the evangelical
vote. He did not need any more votes. He was marking the end of the Civil
War and the beginning of his second term as president. He used the word
"God" 14 times in this speech, which is only 701 words in total.

God is not a figure referred to or a word used in presidential speeches
before Lincoln's time, either. In my own searching through historical
record, I have only found John Quincy Adams—our best-educated, sixth
president—ever to have used it in such a speech. At that, he only used the
word once.

Had Lincoln gone off the deep end here, with his "God," "God" and
more "God"?

Well, yes, he had. He had gone off the political rails and onto the wheels
of the chariots of fire that lift up to heaven. He was willing and able to talk

about the ultimate truth—not just general truth, but God's truth. He was trying to evoke God's truth as to why America had had this terrible civil war going on for so long.

In Lincoln's time it was very unusual for someone in his position to talk about God this way, but he had to get something off his chest and into the people's minds. He had been meditating on this in anguish for several years: *This war—Why, God?! Why?!*

In our current historical situation it is also increasingly problematic to talk about God, either politically or socially. The word and the name of God have been used for some of the more ill-reputed things that nations have done over the past century. Both sides in the world wars of the 20th century used the name of God. Think of Bob Dylan's song *Masters of War*, or *With God on Our Side*.

Lincoln pointed out in his second Inaugural Address that both sides had invoked the name of God during the Civil War.

Today, we are cynical. We easily dismiss the lack of logic in the theory that God could be on two different sides at the same time. Lincoln dismisses that, too. But still he carries on with this God talk.

Not only are we, today, easily cynical about a politician using the name of God, but people don't talk about God much at all in their everyday lives. Only 7 percent of people (according to a *New York Times* report) talk about God regularly and with the people they encounter in a typical week. So that's 93 percent who don't. Even religious people reported that only 13 percent of them would talk about God at least once a week. People are afraid of arguments, of politicized talk, of not wanting to appear weird, too religious or just plain extreme. In fact, in the last 500 years, the use of religious words has fallen off by 50 percent, researchers have found. Words like *love, patience, gentleness, faithfulness, modesty, kindness* and *thankfulness* have half the shelf life they used to have.

In his second Inaugural Address, Lincoln is drawing to an end his spiritual conversation with America. He wants people to know what he has come to know and believe: that it is God's justice that is worked out on the anvil of history.

After that speech, Lincoln told newspaper publisher Thurlow Weed that although the speech would likely wear well over time, he also knew that people did not much like being told that their own purpose and God's purposes could be at loggerheads. People did not want to hear that God really wasn't for the North or the South.

Lincoln was particularly eager to know what Frederick Douglass, the great abolitionist leader, thought of his speech. At first, Douglass was prevented from entering the White House reception due to his race, but Lincoln waved him in through a doorway and asked for his reaction.

Douglass said it was "a sacred effort." Lincoln was pleased.

So, may we try from time to time to engage in spiritual conversations, as did Lincoln, and speak of divine attributes—God's light—to light us down in honor, to the latest generation.

# 16

# Even We Here
# Hold the Power

*"We—even we here—hold the power and bear the responsibility."*

**-Abraham Lincoln**

http://bit.ly/2jCWYpd

**IN THE QUOTE** above, Lincoln graphically underscored two words: *we* and *here*. It is as if he wanted them read aloud with special emphasis: "We here!" Today, we might call this something similar to *The Eternal Now* or *The Power of Now*.

Not only does the printed text of this speech have *we here* in italics, but the phrase "even we here" is set off with em dashes. Lincoln's written speeches often make great use of em dash lines, and "even we here" would have would have rung out, oratorically. However, we also know that because this was a speech to Congress in December of 1862, it would have been read aloud by a Congressional reader and not spoken in person by President Lincoln, as was the custom of the time.

Today we have books such as *The Power of Now*, by Eckhart Tolle, or *The Eternal Now*, by Paul Tillich, but Lincoln was not a 20th century philosopher-theologian. Yet he echoes those writers as he calls Congress, and the nation, to come into the present and to hold power and bear responsibility. This is a high calling—a muscular one—to ethical life.

What was the power and the responsibility that Lincoln was calling Congress to hold and to bear? Nothing less than the hot coals of abolitionists that had been heaped on the heads of the nation for decades. Lincoln is bringing their racial and radical ethics to the feet of Congress, telling them: *Free the slaves*. That is his injunction. It is still early in the Civil War, but Lincoln is indicating, in some way, that that is what will need to be done. *Grant this freedom.* He doubles the ethic by saying: *By freeing them, we free ourselves.*

Lincoln has seen the consequences of slavery and its long history all his life. Throughout his childhood, Lincoln saw slavery morally rotting families and individuals. He knew families that would not let their children play with the children of slave traders. (Slave traders were a moral pariah to everyone, black and white.) The guilt of human and, of course, sexual bondage wracked everyone, even threatening the very civic freedoms that the Constitution had promised the white population. Slavery was enslaving the very principles and values of a great hope on earth: American democracy.

Lincoln is saying: *Save yourselves. Save the slaves. Save us all. Let us find a path to freedom for all. Only then can we find true liberty and justice.*

He concludes this moral challenge by saying that the world will applaud, and God will bless us, if we can do this.

The last paragraph alone, in that speech to Congress, would qualify Lincoln as a president with a spiritual life. It is, at the very least, a sermon. And if it had been all he had ever said about this dark and dreadful ethical burden, it would be a shining light—a beacon in American political and presidential statements. A real and lasting tweet, we could say.

But hang on! There is even more to the sheer glory of Lincoln's spiritual self, words, actions and thoughts.

All of this now-eternal, now-even-we-here language that he is creating—all this freedom-, freedom-, freedom-here-and-now, in our history and for our future—are lines he is writing after he has said something very strange. He had opened this paragraph about ethical responsibility by saying, "Fellow citizen, we cannot escape history."

Any one of Lincoln's friends in Springfield might have declared something like, "Golly, Abe, what do you mean, telling us we cannot escape history? We are slaves to time itself, and now you want us to turn around and act as if we are free—that we have escaped history and time itself and more? You want us to free them, those whom the Fugitive Slave Act says should never escape? Abe, you are one powerfully confounding person!"

Of course, the nation took up Lincoln's paradoxical and confounded imperative. We are bound by time—and we are free to act in moral and just ways.

It would take a biblical theologian to work that out for Abraham Lincoln, and while he read a number of books on theology, he worked it out himself. Therefore, we must do this, also. We, too, can take this paradox that Lincoln presents us—a timeless God in the midst of history—and light down freedom and justice, as did he and as did America, to the latest generation.

# 17

# Four Score and Seven

*"Four score and seven years ago ..."*

-Abraham Lincoln

http://bit.ly/2jCWYWf

**THE QUOTE ABOVE** is, of course, the memorable opening to Lincoln's Gettysburg Address, which he delivered on November 19th, 1863.

Note that he says "four score and seven," rather than "87 years ago." In understanding the spiritual life of Lincoln, there is a reason why he chooses to start with the number *87* and there is a reason why he chooses the archaic "four score and seven." Often, Lincoln thinks and speaks more like a spiritual poet than a rational politician.

At Gettysburg, Lincoln was attempting to invoke the "Spirit of '76," when the banner-raising Declaration of Independence was signed by people with the commitment to risk their lives, fortunes and sacred honor. As Lincoln saw it, 1776 was when the blood of the American Revolution began to flow—and the idea of America was conceived. For him, the nearly mystical idea of a freed and equal people governing themselves was the real origin of America. Those powerful ideas were, Lincoln believed, even more important than the Constitution, which came a decade later.

As Lincoln looked back, he believed that the conception of America— while not exactly an immaculate conception—was much more of a holy idea than a law book. And it is conception and birth that are the metaphors and verbs he used in this speech.

We have two really different frames of mind here: the fever and blood of an ideal versus the debate and ink of a document.

So, Lincoln used biblical language—not arithmetic—to name the value of the moment. "Four score and seven years ago" is how Lincoln, who had memorized much of the Bible, echoes the language of Psalm 90's meditation on the life span of a human being, especially in relation to the eternity of God:

> The days of our years are threescore and ten; and, if by reason
> of strength, they be fourscore years, yet is their strength
> labor and sorrow; for it is soon cut off, and we fly away.

In other words, human life is short—perhaps only 70 years. Even if we do reach 80 years, labor and sorrow will use up our strength. Lincoln did not get to 80 or 70, and nearly all of his labor was in sorrow.

Lincoln could not help himself in casting his comments in biblical tones, because for him, the vocabulary of the holy is what was called for when a battlefield (and all it represented) was being dedicated to the sacrifice of young American warriors. Secularizing forces in our modern Western world have drained our religious traditions of many of their riches, encouraging us to prize material success over spiritual depth. Lincoln was never fooled by that temptation.

As a spiritual poet, Lincoln stood at the cusp of this looming secularization. He was born at the height of what we call, today, "that old-time religion," and his mind was formed in the thought patterns of the Bible first and then the law. So, as he pulled out his little slip of paper and began his address at the battlefield, it was natural for him to reach, first, for the Bible. He looks to the past because that is where biblical authors look as they survey the history of God's people. Lincoln's restless mind was always trying to understand his moment within the grand sweep of history.

At Gettysburg, he does not gain his inspiration from the crowds around him; he does not look to the stars and the trees and the beauties of nature. He looks to history.

Why is looking to history a spiritual thing to do?

History is bigger than we are. History is a driving force, pushing us from behind into a "now" that is colliding with the future. Lincoln's favorite line from Shakespeare was, "There's a divinity that shapes our ends/ Rough hew them how we will."

All of Lincoln's thoughts, words and actions flow from his humility: his sense that he is small and history and God are vast. The sweep of the eternal infinite is the mindset and the vocabulary of a spiritual person.

Lincoln believed that we cannot escape history, but we can take up our responsibility and find, if not our significance, then our honor—even down to the latest generation.

# 18

# Certain Uncertainty

*"These are not ... the days of miracles, and I suppose it will be granted that I am not to expect a direct revelation."*

**-Abraham Lincoln**

http://bit.ly/2jCWZth

**IN THESE WORDS,** President Lincoln is agonizing over the Civil War: why it is going on so long, why it started and why no one can seem to stop it. While he takes responsibility every day (and long into almost every night) for the conduct of his office and the war, he also has a philosopher's mind—and more, he has a biblical language for his thinking.

The words "miracles" and "revelation" he gets from the Bible. He has, since boyhood, read passages from Scripture. Certainly, the parting of the Red Sea for the Hebrew slaves' exodus from Egypt caught his boyish imagination. But, as president, he cannot hope to perform as Moses once did.

Likewise, the word "revelation" is a biblical term—not one philosophers use. Lincoln is realistically noting that he is not going to get the God-given miracle of a direct revelation of God's will and God's way.

So he sits in the dark, without a revelation. This is particularly hard for him because he does not believe in a dark and meaningless world. He has always held that there is "a divinity that shapes our ends/ Rough hew them though we will," as Shakespeare put it. Fate, and then the providence of God, are maxims for him—but maxims with no usable message he can discern.

Lincoln does not believe in the words of *The Battle Hymn of the Republic*, Julia Ward Howe's assertion that God's truth is marching on—Northern-Union-Yankee-style. Nor does Lincoln believe in General Stonewall

Jackson's Southern Calvinism, nor the Confederate seal in Latin, *Deo Vindice*, "God will vindicate."

This is where the greatness of Lincoln emerges. Words can hardly express the significance of how it is that he lives at the crossroads of history and yet admits that he is largely in the dark.

Unlike a dictator or a demagogue, Lincoln does not boast that he knows all the answers—or even the best answers, at that—as he makes his momentous decisions day after day. Lincoln's attitude was not "my way or the highway." Lincoln saw all Americans as somewhat in the dark, sharing the same crossroad. Yet somehow he managed to keep rolling. For example, he saw that an amendment to end slavery would be needed at the end of the war, and he fought mightily to obtain the 13th Amendment.

The title of this chapter states one way to describe Lincoln's spiritual stance: Certain uncertainty.

This spiritual stance is also one that is necessary for democracy. As Henry David Thoreau put it, in a democracy, "truth is always paradoxical." The democratic mind requires us to hold, side by side, seemingly contradictory ideals and ideas—and then to make choices not between good and evil, but between worthwhile but contradictory values. For example, the tension between freedom for all and equality for everyone requires actions and laws that fall short of fulfilling either goal.

In his new book, *A Higher Loyalty*, former FBI director James Comey writes that "… in a healthy organization, doubt is not weakness, it is wisdom, because people are at their most dangerous when they are certain that their cause is just and their facts are right."

English poet John Keats thought that the ability to stand in the midst of uncertainty and not make an exclusive claim on absolute truth was the essence of wisdom. He believed that all of Shakespeare's works celebrated this kind of humble poise. Doubts and mysteries are as important as facts and reason.

Keats pictured some people as behaving similar to the planet Mercury, which he pictured as dashing, busy as a bee, around the Sun. Other people he regarded as distant, like the orange planet Jupiter, slowly revolving around a larger universe. Fast Mercury. Ponderous Jupiter. Lincoln could be Mercurial, a facile shape-shifter, but he was—due to his sorrows—more the ponderous, Jove-like Jupiter.

A recent book on Lincoln's melancholy puts it this way: "Lincoln's clarity came in part from his uncertainty. ... Lincoln cut straight to the contradiction of both sides' assuming that God was on their side."

This writer, Joshua Shenk, concludes, "Viewing Lincoln through the lens of his lifelong melancholy ... he was always inclined to look at the full truth of a situation, assessing both what could be known and what remained in doubt. When times were hard, he had the patience, endurance and vigor to stay in that place of tension."

Uncertainty, mystery and doubt lead to knowledge, which Lord Byron called sorrow—or what Lincoln scholar John Burt calls Lincoln's tragic pragmatism. Such sorrow leads to wisdom, and wisdom leads to an open mind that is able to take decisive action.

In the certain light of uncertainty, Lincoln's quiet fire can light us down in honor—to the latest generation.

# 19

# The River of Love

*"It is true—true indeed I did. I loved the woman dearly and soundly: She was a handsome girl—would have made a good, loving wife ... I did honestly and truly love the girl and think often, often of her now."*

**-Abraham Lincoln, as noted by historian and author David Donald**

http://bit.ly/2jBflec

**IN THE QUOTE** above, Lincoln is speaking of Ann Rutledge, believed to be the first serious romantic interest in his life. When she was lying on her deathbed on August 25, 1835, she specifically insisted that she see Abe Lincoln.

The quote represents Lincoln's words as remembered by an old friend, Isaac Cogdal, in the days following Lincoln's election as president. Historians increasingly credit the role of Ann Rutledge in his life, although the historical record about her is relatively sparse.

As we have been focusing on Lincoln's spiritual life, we have tended to downplay his political and historical lives. Of course, it is an act of imagination to even suggest that one person has three distinct lives, so let's continue along this line for a moment. After years of research, I believe that Lincoln's spiritual life would have been remarkable whether he was president or not. We don't really need his historical fame to value his spiritual life—although we might never have heard of this spiritual pioneer had he not also become president. Can you imagine Lincoln as a legendary frontier character without his presidency? Perhaps his wit and wisdom would have been carried down in songs and folk tales. Perhaps his stepmother would have written a memoir of her tall, exceptional stepson.

Yet this act of our imagination is appropriate when portraying a spiritual life, as it is in the very nature of a spiritual being that he or she is more than merely a material being. A saint is not a saint because he or she is rich and famous; we value spiritual life regardless of wealth or fame.

You don't have to be an historian to see the blooming of Lincoln's life-spirit in the few years he lived in New Salem, Illinois. There, Lincoln rooms in the Rutledge Tavern and befriends the tavern owner's daughter, Ann. Lincoln, in his early 20s at this time, is in many ways exploding out of the limitations of his family of origin. He is away from his father for the first time. He is invited into a man's intellectual club. He reads Shakespeare and Byron and Burns in his free time. He becomes a favorite dinner guest of older widows in the area. He runs for a local office and is defeated, but gets almost every single vote in his new little town. He surveys the local Sangamon River for potential steamboat travel.

The image of the river is important here. In the old Henry Fonda movie about Lincoln, directed by John Ford, the director shows the local river flowing along as the thematic visual background in several important scenes. One is when he is walking and talking with Ann Rutledge. In another scene, he is beginning to fall in love with America itself and is deciding to become involved in politics. The image of the river, as it flows through Lincoln's life, becomes an archetype of romantic love. In discovering personal intimacy for the first time in our lives, our minds begin to see that one particular person can hold universal value. That is the spiritual leap that love requires. It is not logical or reasonable, but it is completely persuasive. When people fall in love, they end up easily feeling like they love the world. That is the key to the spirituality of love, and it is abundantly evident in young Lincoln.

In the summer of 1835, both he and Ann Rutledge are besieged by a terrible weather system. (Lincoln's feelings often were triggered by extreme weather. Snowstorms in the winter were key to the depressions he suffered.) The year 1835 was one of the hottest in Illinois history, and it rained, they said, every day that summer. In fact, it was the flooding of the family well that most likely gave Ann Rutledge typhoid fever and caused her death.

Love is both the great awakener of the imagination and, sometimes, the cause of its melancholic morbidity. Lincoln's mind is aflame with grief and poetical vision after Ann's death. He is as obsessed, as any lover would be.

He tells an older female friend, Mrs. Bennett Abell, that he cannot "bare the idea of its raining on her grave."

This is not the language of a material and practical man. This is the soulful vision of a spiritual being who has been lost and found—and then lost again—by love.

Of course, this all requires a leap of imagination: disrobing the presidential Lincoln and stripping away all of the presidential glory, to try to envision him as the raw-boned, spiritual archetype of a lover.

Years later, Lincoln read Ralph Waldo Emerson's injunction that a person needs to follow nature and dive into the river of life—perhaps Lincoln even heard it firsthand from the great essayist.

Lincoln certainly embodied that idea. We can follow Lincoln's life as the river of love continued to flow in him, widening from romantic love to his love of an entire nation—a passion that flows down to us, even to the latest generation.

# 20

# Women on Lincoln

*"Abe was the best boy I ever saw or ever expect to see."*

**-Sarah Bush Lincoln**

http://bit.ly/2jCX00j

**THE QUOTE ABOVE** is what Abraham Lincoln's stepmother, Sarah Bush, said about him after his tragic death. Of her, Lincoln had once written: "No man could love a mother more than he loved her."

Along with the words of praise and love between this stepmother and stepson, what can we learn about the spiritual life of Lincoln from what women said to him or about him?

We know that history is being rewritten to right the many wrongs of traditional "his"-story. One small way to do that is to look at what women had to say about Lincoln, even though Lincoln was clearly a 19th century male in many ways—certainly a patriarchal, if kindly, husband.

Let's start with a reported conversation between Marilyn Monroe and the poet and Lincoln biographer Carl Sandburg. Monroe reportedly told Sandburg that she had always wished that Abraham Lincoln had been her father.

We also know that the renowned muckraking journalist Ida Tarbell not only brought down John D. Rockefeller's Standard Oil monopoly with her massive research, but she reignited the interest in Lincoln biography with her two-volume work at the turn of the last century.

Tarbell wrote that she was so moved by Lincoln that she returned to America from a long stay in France, saying that, "My country's problems are my problems." She took up responsibility for the dark times that resulted from America's Gilded Age. The spirit of Lincoln, by her own admission, helped her to do something about righting America's many wrongs.

From Lincoln's own time, there is a little-known essay about him by Harriet Beecher Stowe, author of *Uncle Tom's Cabin*. Some people also claim that Lincoln was to have said to her, at the White House, "So, you're the little lady that started this great big war?" I am not so sure about that, but I have come across a quote from a regular newspaper column Stowe wrote during the war in which she praised Lincoln for his feminine qualities. Lincoln was such a man's man, in so many ways, that we wonder: What did she mean?

Well, she had a metaphor—an image for her meaning. She was praising Lincoln for his strength of purpose, his steadfastness, his predictable reliability—all strengths desirable in a president. The image that she had in mind was a steel cable. The way she pictured it, the cable was firmly and securely fastened at one end but re-attachable and movable at the other end. Like such a cable, Stowe saw Lincoln as strong but flexible—and she described those strengths as feminine. You can imagine that she is likely contrasting him with other famous men who were identified by their ideological rigidity and bull-headed refusal to change to meet new situations.

Stowe was right in her assessment. This pragmatic adaptability is certainly a characteristic of Lincoln, who once said, "My policy is to have no policy."

Lincoln was not a rigid man, just a strong man. His flexibility drew criticism from other men who regarded it as, essentially, passivity. Today, of course, some historians praise this characteristic of his nature and see it as essential to the "democratic mind"—a mind that exercises paradox, ambiguity and flexibility without abandoning principles.

Throughout these chapters, we have met many women who encountered Lincoln and were impressed with him, including the Quaker minister Eliza Gurney. Even long after his death, a modern movie star like Marilyn Monroe could respond to his remarkable spirit. May that spirit guide us, too, in honor—to the latest generation.

# 21

# Trailing Clouds of Goodness

*"Every man is said to have his peculiar ambition. Whether it be true or not, I can say for one that I have no other so great as that of being truly esteemed of my fellow men, by rendering myself worthy of their esteem."*

**-Abraham Lincoln**

http://bit.ly/2jCX0xl

**ABRAHAM LINCOLN WAS** 23 years old when he wrote the quote above. He was making a newspaper announcement from the little town of New Salem, reporting that he was a candidate to the Illinois General Assembly. The year was 1832.

Lincoln lost that election—his first. Yet he always had a peculiar mixture of humility and ambition. He wanted desperately to be remembered. His partner said, of his ambition, that it was like a "little engine." Lincoln wanted to be remembered for being good and he wanted to be worthy of the esteem of others.

When we think of spiritual figures we admire, we often assume that they are spiritual because they are selfless and giving. Lincoln's spiritual life shows us something different: someone who was able to make willing sacrifice but who also wanted to be remembered forever. Virtue was his path to glory, and he wanted both virtue and glory.

In a law lecture to young men, Lincoln shared that he, himself, had resolved to be an honest lawyer. If it was not possible to be both honest and a lawyer, then he would resolve to be honest. In Lincoln's mind, virtue trumped fame.

Now, here is how an ethical life can be a spiritual life. There is a theory that states that spiritual things are eternal. In 1913, Boris Pasternak wrote a philosophical essay about this theory, called *Symbolism and Immortality*.

We know Pasternak as the man who won the Noble Prize in literature for his novel *Doctor Zhivago.*

Pasternak wrote that all the sounds we hear and the colors we see correspond to objective vibrations of sound and light. Symbols, he thought, have eternal objective qualities, and it is for this that his character, Doctor Zhivago, lives. Dr. Zhivago lives and loves for something more than the political revolution going on around him. His goal in life is like Lincoln's goal—to live for something so good that participation in it will last forever. Pasternak called this the "suprapersonal quality" of light and sound, and it is through our participation in these objective vibrations that our human happiness comes.

The idea sounds reasonable. This is, perhaps, why we listen to music: because music connects us to something greater and more lasting than our own personal lives and makes our individual lives worth living. This may be similar to Rudolf Steiner's ideas about colors and plants and things.

Pasternak concluded something about life that Lincoln sought. As Pasternak wrote, "the happiness of existence" is experienced as immortal—like what artists create. Then, to quote him again, an artist strives so that "other people centuries after ... might experience, through his works, something approaching the personal and innermost form of his original sensations."

I had an experience of Lincoln like this once—an experience that Pasternak suggests in his essay, saying, "... every person leaves behind him a part of that undying, generic subjectivity which he possessed during his lifetime and with which he participated in the history of mankind's existence."

While living in southern Indiana, I visited Lincoln's boyhood home—the one where he had lived from age 9 to 21. One summer day, I walked a path from where his log cabin had been, past his mother's grave and toward the museum that was built there. I was standing near where Lincoln would, as a boy, have taken a bucket and gone for water, with his cat following him through the woods. In the sunlight on the leaves of those trees and in the air around and above, I felt the palpable goodness of Abraham Lincoln. At that moment, I thought that some people contain such concentrations of goodness that they leave some of it as a real spiritual presence—wherever they go.

Lincoln's life now, like a living novel, might carry for us a light and sound to guide us—down to the latest generation.

# 22

# Faithful Over a Little

*"If any man thinks I am a coward, let him test it."*

**-Abraham Lincoln**

http://bit.ly/2jCX28r

**IN THE QUOTE** above, 23-year-old Abraham Lincoln challenged an angry group of men who wanted to kill an old Indian man named Jack.

This may have been the most important turning point in Lincoln's life, both in terms of his character—its spiritual core—and in terms of practical political consequences. While he certainly did not take this courageous stand for political reasons, he was nevertheless a captain in the state militia at the time, fighting in what was called the Black Hawk War. Almost every major political figure in Lincoln's career in Illinois turns out to have been a member of that militia, and would have heard of Lincoln's noble and principled stance. They later became his colleagues in the legislature, the law and then in national political campaigns, for the rest of his life.

I have invited you to consider the core of Lincoln's spiritual life—to appreciate how outstanding his spirit was, regardless of his future presidential greatness. Even if he had wound up as a nearly forgotten frontiersman, we can imagine that Lincoln's spirit would have been legendary among the pioneers around him. In other words, as we remove the presidential robes from Lincoln to ponder the bare-boned man within that office, we are astonished to see that he often seemed to embody Jesus's teachings. In the situation with Jack, for example, he was demonstrating his faithfulness over a little—before he became faithful over a lot.

Lincoln did this by first stepping into the role of the warrior. Secular life and sacred life meet in the spiritual archetype of the warrior. Lincoln's spiritual identity begins with that calling and then comes to flower as he serves as a captain in the Black Hawk War, in 1832.

Being a warrior is a calling: It asks that the person go beyond the boundaries of the self and ego to protect or to destroy others for the purpose of community security. It is, in essence, a service to others. Before becoming a militia man, Lincoln had only been a family member and a store clerk. His self was enlarging as he took on the spirit of the warrior.

This is how—in his role as a captain—Lincoln meets a runaway Indian. Keep in mind that this is at a moment when his troops are at war with Indians.

Here we have a story that embodies one of the most dramatic teachings of Jesus: when he said, "as you have done it unto the least of these, my brethren, you have done it unto me."

Many of us might say, *Oh I'll be good when I am famous.* Lincoln's life, on the contrary, gives evidence that he did (and practiced) good whether he was famous or not.

As we shall see, Lincoln is guided by his compassion and his character in the case of the old renegade Indian. This is his spiritual silhouette—a profile in courage.

First, we see Lincoln defending the life of one human being, considered then to be only a savage in the spring of 1832.

Then, 30 years later and in the fall of 1862, Lincoln shows the same courage, compassion and character. The spiritual life of Lincoln in 1862 turns out to be identical to his brave stance in that much earlier conflict, three decades prior. In 1862, as president, Lincoln personally saves the lives of 265 Indians—Sioux, from Minnesota—and maybe the lives of hundreds more, including women and children, as over 1,500 were originally arrested.

As this story unfolds, it is important to recall that Lincoln, as historian David Donald writes, "… had little acquaintance with Indians. In general, like most whites of his generation, he considered the Indians a barbarous people who were a barrier to progress." Nevertheless, Lincoln works mightily to practice the Golden Rule and to enact the Christ-like spirit of attending to the lives of the "least of these" (Matthew 25:40).

From the point of view of spiritual life, the 30 years that had passed between Lincoln's bold stand to save one Native American life to his bold stand to save 265 is but a twinkling of an eye. Time is irrelevant in life when eternity is the measure. Jesus's quote about the "least of these" is a saying about the status of one's immortal soul, one's eternal destiny.

The timelessness of spiritual life and value is what stands out in these two stories about Lincoln. The words of Jesus speak to an equality of humanity that truly fits Lincoln's view. As a young captain in the Black Hawk War, he also is taking up the "warrior code," the spiritual archetype of the warrior who takes on Jesus's claim that greater love hath no man than to lay down his life for his friends. Lincoln is willing to risk that. Lincoln adds, to this nobility of sacrifice, the added Christian value that the friends need not be important friends, but maybe even of the least of all other people— in Lincoln's world, the status of Indians and slaves.

We instinctively admire people—anonymous or famous, real or imagined—who can stand up against angry mob violence. In the novel *To Kill A Mockingbird*, we see Atticus Finch stop a lynch mob at the jailhouse door. In real history, we see former Maine Governor Joshua Lawrence Chamberlain stand on the Augusta capital steps to defend the electoral process against a dangerous mob in 1880.

Lincoln had a great deal of power in the fall of 1862. Starving Sioux Indians had been told to eat grass (or worse) while they were awaiting their recompense for land from the U.S. government. They rioted and killed more than 350 white settlers—the largest massacre of whites by Indians in American history. One thousand, five hundred Indians were arrested, including women and children. Three hundred and three were to be executed. If those executions were not carried out, the governor of Minnesota warned that angry whites would exterminate all Indians in Minnesota. The governor and his allies used terms like "maniacs" and "wild beasts" to describe these men and women.

Lincoln stood on principles. Reviewing the documents on the 303, he saved all but 38. This still was the largest mass execution in American history, but it might have been horrifically larger without Lincoln's intervention.

In 1832, Abraham Lincoln had very little power. He was the locally elected captain of a militia assigned to secure the border of Illinois against a similarly starving band of displaced Native Americans, including the elderly, women and children. Indians were not popular at this time. "Red lives" did not matter. When Lincoln and his men encountered one lone man, named in history only as Jack, they found he had a letter in his hand from an American general, vouching for him. Lincoln, who had lost his own grandfather—another Captain Abraham Lincoln—to Indian snipers, could easily have sought revenge. But blood revenge is not in the spiritual code of the warrior, though often the temptation is there.

Tempers flared in Lincoln's ragtag militia. His men were saying things like, "By God, we have come to fight Indians and we intend to do so!" And, "This is cowardly on your part, Lincoln."

That is when he declared: "If any man thinks I am a coward, let him test it."

No one did.

This is where spiritual life has consequence for leadership: in virtue and values. Self-centeredness is the rot at the core of a failing civilization. Transcendent values—especially self-sacrifice—are the gold at the spiritual center of any person, great or small.

In the light of such spiritual truth we, too, can be lighted down in honor—to the latest generation.

# 23

# Of Planting and Washing Away

*"It wouldn't be easy to forget that Saturday afternoon in corn-planting time when other boys dropped the seed-corn into all the rows in the big seven-acre field—and Abe dropped the pumpkin seed. He dropped two seeds at every other hill and every other row."*

**-Carl Sandburg**

http://bit.ly/2jBflLe

**THE QUOTE ABOVE** is actually a short scene from Carl Sandburg's biographical account of the young "shirt-tail boy"—Abe Lincoln. (By the way, "shirt-tail" is an Appalachian term meaning something like "disheveled, young and poor," and seems to be a term also favored by contemporary author Stephen King.) The specific detail here—two seeds in every other hill and row—validates this as one of Lincoln's first memories. David Herbert Donald, a Harvard historian whose work focused on Abraham Lincoln and the Civil War, also recorded the details of the two seeds, every other hill and row, just as the folksy and poetic Carl Sandburg did.

A W.B. Yeats poem that mentions seed plantings comes to mind, too, as we talk about Lincoln's childhood:

> I will arise and go now, and go to Innisfree
>
> And a small cabin build there, of clay and wattles made;
>
> Nine bean rows will I have …

The annual tedium of numbered seed plantings sparked Yeats' poetic yearning for the Irish past—a kind of Walden-like, simple, natural vision of the past. Yeats liked to call the place "the deep heart's core." This tiny detail of Lincoln's history takes us to the archetypal ground of spiritual birth: nature and childhood.

This account of Lincoln is one of the earliest looks we have into his spiritual origins. This is primal ground, like his mother's lap and the Bible, in which we see him—and we see him seeing both himself and life.

Historian Doris Kearns Godwin recently said that Lincoln may have simply been born with a generous spirit. But it is in his first experiences with life and land that we see his deep-hearted, generous core take on its melancholy shape.

There is a reason why Lincoln would be able to recall such a particular Saturday afternoon of pumpkin-seed planting: because the next Sunday there was a hard rain, and his pumpkin seeds (along with his father's corn plantings) were washed away.

No lesson in the nature of life is more fundamental to Lincoln than this: the lesson of impermanence. The one poem Lincoln recited all his life was written by William Knox, and called *Mortality*. This poem proclaims the foolishness of human pride, and opens:

> O why should the spirit of mortal be proud?
> Like a fast-flitting meteor, a fast-flying cloud,
> A flash of the lightning, a break of the wave,
> He passes from life to his rest in the grave.

The poem above describes the same ephemeral life that is taught by the winds that blow apart a Buddhist sand painting. In the case of the Buddhist painting, the elaborate sand art is created and then it is blown away, symbolizing the sands of time and awakening the deep heart's core of compassion.

Lincoln was intimately acquainted with nature's lessons on humility and the limits of human work and pride. During his lifetime, Lincoln also recalled a curious fact about this particular time of flooding at his family's farm. He noticed that the rain that washed everything away did not come down in the valley, where they were planting—not a drop. It only rained up in the knobby hills, and then the flooding waters flowed downward. Lincoln's noting this suggests that he saw it as at least ironic that the rains spared the field—only to wash it out another way. To a little boy, such irony could seem very frustrating, if not downright unjust.

It was at this beautiful, small farm in Kentucky, a place called Knob Creek, that two other spirit-shaping events happened, too. One was that

Lincoln's baby brother, Thomas, died there when Lincoln was 3. There is a tombstone there with the simple initials T. L. (Thomas Lincoln was their father's namesake). The other pivotal event that occurred in Knob Creek was that Lincoln came very close to drowning in the fast-moving stream. Only the quick action of his friend, in extending a long branch to Lincoln, saved his life.

Seeing life so swiftly taken away, seeing planting washed away, almost drowning—all of these events become the ground of Lincoln's very being.

One thinks of the early parable of Jesus, about the sower who went out to sow. For this sower, some of his seed fell upon the dry ground, some among the rocks, some on poor soil and some washed away. In Jesus's astringent story, only one in four plantings survived.

In such a teaching from the natural world, we, too—in our own spiritual life—can, like Lincoln, be lightened down in honor—even to the latest generation.

# 24

# Thanksgiving and Praise

*"I do therefore invite my fellow citizens in every part of the United States, and also those who are at sea and those who are sojourning in foreign lands, to set apart and observe the last Thursday of November next, as a day of Thanksgiving and Praise to our beneficent Father who dwelleth in the Heavens."*

**-Abraham Lincoln, October 3, 1863**

http://bit.ly/2jBfmig

**TODAY, WE MAY** not think twice about Lincoln's creation of the national Thanksgiving holiday. Yet federal holidays were different back when Lincoln was president, so it was surprising that he decided to set aside a day for the nation to engage in what was considered religious activities—giving thanks and praise. Most religious holidays, even worldwide, were not created by rulers, kings or presidents.

There were only two federal holidays observed when Lincoln named the last Thursday in November as a day of national thanksgiving. There was the Fourth of July—the national birthday—and the birthday of George Washington. Christmas wasn't a national day; Puritan Pilgrims had hated it. Lincoln once held a Cabinet meeting on Christmas Day. Charles Dickens' 1843 tale, *A Christmas Carol*, was still percolating a renewed interest in the holiday during Lincoln's time, with its images of hot mulled wine and port, or "Smoking Bishop."

How could Lincoln get away with this blend of religious activity and national custom in his 1863 declaration? The answer is quite simple, really: It was because of Americans' unique way of life. On the one hand, we, as Americans, constitutionally separate church and state; on the other hand, we are passionate about completely mixing religion and politics. We limit the role of government in our lives and yet we accept all sorts of governmental intrusions—like a presidential holiday.

This mix of sacred and secular is yet another reason why the spiritual life of Lincoln is so real and relevant. Lincoln, almost like a high priest, asked his fellow citizens to set aside a day for the traditionally religious activities of giving thanks and offering praise. Throughout the Civil War, both Lincoln and his opposite, President of the Confederate States Jefferson Davis, instituted national days of either fasting for sins and atonement or giving thanks for the celebration of victories.

The editor of a famous women's magazine in Lincoln's era had been trying, for several years, to convince an American president to institute a national day of thanksgiving. Lincoln seized this idea, believing it to be a way to bring the nation back together as the war was coming to an end.

But what is missing in Lincoln's declaration? He never mentions Pilgrims or Indians. He makes no reference to Christ or churches. He never even makes a comment about turkeys. In fact, Lincoln only asks people to adopt a meditative, grateful state of mind in their praise—no matter where they are or who they are.

Essentially, Lincoln is, through his declaration, inviting Southerners to reclaim their American status. He also is asking people at sea or sojourners in foreign lands—Americans all—to honor this day.

Lincoln is not making a small point here. He is directing our eyes to a far grander vision of America. He is not arguing that America arises out of the soil; it is not the land that makes us American. It's a mindset. Americans are not a race or a tribe. To Lincoln, Americans are a people who have received a great gift: a free nation with self-government. Lincoln invites us to acknowledge that Americans did not create this free nation on their own; in Lincoln's mind, a divine assistance made it possible. At the same time, he asks us to acknowledge what he calls our *perversity*—the ways we have not lived up to the blessings we have received.

Lincoln, as an American, was easily able to take on a religious role in a political setting. In fact, he had been mixing them together all his life. As a boy, he would go to church with his parents. He was the sexton and candle keeper, and his father had made the pulpit by hand. After church services, Lincoln would stand on a tree stump and comically imitate the preacher and his sermon, much to the glee of his friends. Lincoln said that he liked preachers who looked like they were swatting at bees! As a young lawyer he gave speeches against drinking, asking people to forgive drinkers and not accuse them of being sinners. Instead, he encouraged others to acknowledge something: *There, but for the grace of God, go I.* Lincoln gave another speech in which he made George Washington into an almost Christ-like figure, describing his grave as sacred turf and his name as one that must absolutely be honored—and the Constitution as something that is as sacred as the church.

We know that Lincoln relied upon the disciplines of science and reason, and we also know that he did not join a church. Yet his whole life can only be fully understood when we also see the religious dynamic of who he was and what he did, such as creating a national holiday for all to enjoy.

As 19th century German philosopher Francis Grund once put it, "[an American's] country is in his understanding; he carries it with him wherever he goes ... his home is wherever he finds minds congenial with his own."

This is why the idea of America is so important to Lincoln: because it is in our minds—and in the congenial thoughts we share with others—that we find our home and our homeland. It is in that spirit, that idea, that we, too, can be lighted down in honor—even to the latest generation.

# 25

# A Holy Pulpit

*"When I see a man preach, I like to see him fightin' bees!"*

**-Abraham Lincoln**

http://bit.ly/2jCX3cv

**HAVE YOU EVER** seen anyone fighting bees? Waving their arms, jumping up and down, shouting?

As a boy, Lincoln saw his share of emotional preachers—and he probably also saw his share of bees, both around hives and in the woods near his home. He understood spells of violent frenzy and was both amused and impressed by them.

Lincoln's parents, Tom and Nancy, were serious about their Free Baptist church. They left one church and helped start another because they believed that the Gospel included a rejection of slavery. Tom Lincoln built the pulpit of their new church, and Abe volunteered for a role much like a sexton. (We know this because of a small, signed note found in the crevice of the logs that made up the walls of the church with his tally of the candles he was tending.)

There are two main things to remember about Lincoln and preachers: one, that as a boy, he made fun of them; and two, that as a man, he sought them out. Both the amusement and the allure tell us true things about Abraham Lincoln and his spiritual life.

First, the way that Lincoln made fun of preachers was through a type of impersonation. After church, he would gather his young friends around, stand on a tree stump and re-preach the sermon—with, of course, comic exaggerations. This was no small sign of his free spirit, his individuality, his independence. This was also a sign of his verbal brilliance, as he could often remember and imitate the preacher perfectly.

But if imitation is the sincerest form of flattery, Lincoln was also really getting "inside" the message of the minister. While he rejected emotionally oppressive Christianity—remember, he never was baptized and never joined any church as a professing member—he also learned the power of religious words; of holy words.

The second thing to recall about Lincoln and preachers was that, when two of his sons died as boys, Lincoln sought out different Presbyterian preachers for serious guidance and help. He actively solicited their pastoral care for his broken heart, as well as theological conversation about the ways of God through suffering and death. We know that Lincoln once read a 600-page book written by his Illinois minister. In Washington, he was very drawn to the preaching and the presence of Phineas Densmore Gurley, who became his minister.

It is interesting to think about those first preachers Lincoln heard as a boy. They were, in likelihood, very free-thinking. They were traveling preachers, not governed by strict denominational authority. They could preach from their consciences. They also experienced long hours of quiet contemplation with nature as they traveled from town to town.

These preachers were more like Johnny Appleseed—who was, himself, a Gospel preacher—or John James Audubon, an early neighbor of Lincoln's. They were also more educated than most of the people whom Lincoln would meet as a boy.

In his second Inaugural Address, Lincoln sounded very much like a preacher: his magnificent oratory exhorted Americans to recognize a national guilt for slavery and implored them to be merciful. His was not a bully pulpit, but more of a holy pulpit.

Abraham Lincoln was a spiritual man, and his spirit continues to teach and to preach—even down to the latest generation.

# 26

# The Rest of the Story

*"The fiery trial through which we pass, will light us down, in honor or dishonor, to the latest generation."*

**-Abraham Lincoln, 1862**

http://bit.ly/2jBfjmA

**THE QUOTE ABOVE** contains Lincoln's words from the end of his State of the Union Address, presented in December of 1862. This was a long speech, with lots of reports and facts and figures about the status of the government. Yet anger, uncertainty, fear and passion were nearly overwhelming everyone in the country—Northerners and Southerners alike.

The Civil War was heating up to become the cauldron we now know it became. So, at the end of his long report to Congress, Lincoln closes with a desperate plea: *Can we all do better?*

Then he pens his inspirational prose about fiery trial and honor. Consider the biblical echoes as he says, "the dogmas of the quiet past are inadequate to the stormy present." His tone is almost a prayer, ending with: "The way is plain, peaceful, generous, just—a way which, if followed, the world will forever applaud, and God must forever bless."

There is a personal reason why the words "fiery trial" came to Lincoln as he wrote the end of this speech: A little more than a month before, he'd had one of the most unusual and moving meetings of his long spiritual journey. As described earlier, a famous Quaker woman, Eliza Gurney, had come to his study in the White House with a group of other Quaker women.

Lincoln was getting used to religious people coming to him and telling him what God wanted him to do. But Gurney said that she hadn't come to preach to Lincoln. She had come to offer him spiritual comfort and encouragement as he took upon himself the burden of leading a broken nation. And then, of all things, she got down on her knees in front of the president—you can just imagine the bustling skirts—and prayed for him. She prayed for Abraham Lincoln.

We know that Lincoln remembered this meeting because of a word he used in a letter to Gurney a year later. He recalls the spiritual comfort of their meeting and he acknowledges that, yes, it is a fiery trial through which they are all passing.

Why did he phase it that way? He writes "yes" in his letter because she had used that very turn of phrase with him. He is saying, *Why, yes, it is just as you said when you were here.*

And why did Gurney use those words? She, like Lincoln, was a student of the Bible and knew those words from the New Testament. "Fiery trial" comes from the epistle First Peter, a letter to the new and suffering Christians. In First Peter chapter 4, verse 12, it is written: "Beloved, do not be surprised at the fiery trail when it comes upon you to test you, as though something strange were happening to you."

That would have spoken to Lincoln directly, becoming particularly memorable by the heart-opening praying that Gurney offered so dramatically. She was calling upon the memory of the trials and tribulations of the early followers of Jesus. What could faith and hope be like for them, in a time of radical cultural devastation?

So, Lincoln writes to her: "We are indeed going through a great trial—a fiery trial."

Historian Doris Kearns Godwin, in her book on four presidents who lead through turbulent times, states that good presidents change and learn as they suffer hardship. They become more generous and more able through the suffering of the country and their own lives. She mentions Franklin Roosevelt's first years of the onslaught of polio and the loss of the use of his legs.

There is a hope that comes only through grief and hard times. Feminist writer Rebecca Solnit recently wrote about the political upheaval in our country that has occurred over the last couple of years; about trying to find hope in the midst of grief among the many Americans who are heartbroken over our leadership.

In a Lincoln-esque way, Solnit writes, "The sorrow and hurt, the sleeplessness and indignation, are not themselves powers, but they testify to a public-spirited population that may be able to take the country back."

And, in just such a Lincoln-esque, transformative spirit, we, too, might be able to practice hope in grief and be lighted in honor—down to the latest generation.

# 27

# The Better Angels of Our Nature

*"I am loth to close. We are not enemies, but friends. We must not be enemies. Though passion may have strained, it must not break our bonds of affection. The mystic chords of memory, stretching from every battlefield, and patriot grave, to every living heart and hearth-stone, all over this broad land, will yet swell the chorus of the Union, when again touched, as surely they will be, by the better angels of our nature."*

**-Abraham Lincoln, from his first Inaugural Address**

http://bit.ly/2jBfmPi

**MANY PEOPLE THROUGHOUT** our history have known the phrase, "the better angels of our nature"; Lincoln didn't invent that string of words, and in fact, I have seen it in the text of one of his schoolbooks.

The idea of better angels lets you know—kind of through the back door—that there are worse angels. For better and for worse.

In the Calvinistic religion of Lincoln's youth, the worse angels of our nature were something that—well, he'd heard a whole lot about them in church.

Note that in his first Inaugural Address he uses the word "loth," an archaic spelling of *loath*, to close this speech. That's a humble, almost agonizing, way to end a speech. Like the old doo-wop song, he was calling out: "Stay! Just a little bit longer."

There is a poignant yearning in his words. Lincoln can see so clearly that, after he stops talking—at some point soon—the guns of war will start firing. And they did, just a few weeks later.

It is very Lincoln-esque for him to recall the phrase, "the better angels of our nature." Angelic imagery was big in the 19th century, and Lincoln used it. But he kept a cold eye on our bad angels, as well.

Lincoln wrote a poem in 1840 about what he called the "sorrowing angels," whose mournful, song-like cries he could hear early in the morning. The climactic verse states:

Air held her breath; trees with the spell

Seemed sorrowing angels round,

Whose swelling tears in dewdrops fell

Upon the listening ground.

In that poem, he was specifically recalling the angry and mournful cries of his childhood friend, Matthew Gentry, who had gone violently mad: howling like a dog, physically attacking his parents, needing to be chained and caged. In his memory Lincoln hears a mournful song, like sorrowful angels flowing through the early-morning trees. You might think that, with the mad and violent war coming, he would end his speech by reciting more of these mourning songs of sorrowing angels. But he did not.

It is a testimony to his optimistic faith in human reason and human goodness that Lincoln does not trail off into echoes of Edgar Allen Poe. His original poem certainly veered in that direction.

In preparing his first Inaugural Address, Lincoln had some options regarding how to talk about angels. Humble as he was, Lincoln submitted the draft of his speech to his new Secretary of State, William Seward—the man everyone thought should have been president, including Seward himself. He gave Lincoln 49 changes in the speech; Lincoln accepted 27. One had to do with angels, and what Lincoln did with Seward's angels tells us a lot about his spiritual life.

Both Lincoln and Seward were used to working with images of music and angels. In Seward's metaphor, the mystic chords, some music will proceed from battlefields and graves around the country, passing—somehow—through hearts and hearths and then, in some way, there will be a harmonizing. We are not sure what will harmonize—the music, the hearts or the hearths. The wording is vague. But what did Seward propose would make this harmony happen? Well, he asserted that there was a national guardian angel who would breathe upon the people. That would do it.

Frankly, Lincoln had more guts than this—and a clearer vision of what would happen. In Lincoln's edition—the one the world heard—the mystic chords are not just of some kind of music; they are mystic chords of memory. They do not simply proceed or arise, but instead stretch, from battlefield and grave, until a heartfelt, living connection is made to every living heart and hearthstone. And for Lincoln it will be the people's memory that will swell the music, not some national guardian angel. It's not just a blending harmony that will occur—some version of "can't we just all get along somehow?"—but memory that becomes actual chords of the Union. That's Lincoln's crowning political idea: union.

Upon reaching unity—that is when human hearts will surely be touched, Lincoln acclaims. It is not breathed-upon, ancient music that will somehow harmonize people; rather, it is the actual shared memory of the idea of the Union—the idea of America—that will touch every living heart. This, he believes, will touch the better angels of our nature.

This isn't outside inspiration; it is internal transformation. We are not remembering ancient music. Memory *is* our music.

Lincoln used to call his biological, but long-deceased mother "my sweet angel mother." *Angel* and *human*, as words, could go together. Lincoln reasoned that that is how it could be. He held the memory of the Union with the memory of his mother. His hope was a conviction that it would be, sooner or later, how it would be with us. Surely we will again be touched by what is better, more angelic, about us.

This, then, was a good Inaugural Address, expressing long-term hope in the midst of a dark time. We can, from the spiritual life of Abraham Lincoln, have it guide us—down to the latest generation.

# Like an Eagle

*"… a government like ours … It gave the young eagle scope for his wings."*
**-Joshua Speed, a friend of Abraham Lincoln**

http://bit.ly/2jBfnmk

**THE QUOTE ABOVE** came from Joshua Speed, who was among the truest friends Lincoln ever made. In 1887, more than two decades after Lincoln's death, Speed penned some of his feelings and thoughts about his remarkable prairie friend.

Speed uses an image, a symbol—the eagle—to describe his friend's great power and his interaction with society and civilization. Government was the wind; Lincoln, the eagle's wing. Lincoln, in his perspective, was no more a self-made man than an eagle is able to fly without air.

In a very early form of religion, called animism, the natural world was believed to be full of spirits. Many people of the modern age are returning to that sacred view. Animism is rich with symbols, such as animals that carry spiritual power and meaning. So it is not surprising that Lincoln's friend might see in the eagle something parallel to his friend, the late president.

It is interesting to note that Speed did not vote for Lincoln, and that he was a slave owner. Yet both men had hearts bigger than history, and that is what a symbol can point to: values and meaning beyond the material world.

The eagle, as a spiritual symbol, is used for nations, empires and even church pulpits and lecterns. The image is found in Psalm 103:

> Bless the Lord, O my soul,
>
> and do not forget all his benefits—
>
> who forgives all your iniquity …
>
> who crowns you with steadfast love and mercy,

who satisfies you with good as long as you live

so that your youth is renewed like the eagle's.

An ancient myth held that, even with its wings on fire, an eagle could plunge into the ocean and come up with new wings, renewed.

The prophet Isaiah hoped that elder people could be like the eagle, and says, in chapter 40: "Even youths shall faint and be weary, and young men shall fall exhausted, but they who wait on the Lord shall renew their strength, they shall mount up with wings like eagles, they shall run and not be weary, they shall walk and not faint."

Animal images as religious symbols are powerful—and dangerous. Human ideas about ethics don't apply in the animal world. Spiritual life often takes us beyond simple ideas of good and bad. All the people can't be all good all the time—and Lincoln wasn't, either. Lincoln was thought of as a monster by some, including an editor of the *Belfast Republican Journal* who compared Lincoln with the ancient warrior Hannibal from Carthage, who piled up the skulls of the dead youth as a monument to himself.

But like the eagle, Lincoln had a high-horizon view of life, including political life. He made decisions that defy easy definition as good or evil, but all for a great good that he believed he saw.

On his flight, Lincoln had enough distance not to hate the South nor think that the North was completely good. When Teddy Roosevelt used Lincoln as his model for the values of his new nationalism and his fight against the robber barons, Teddy clarified: *We do not hate wealth*. It was only unfairness, rigged inequality, that Teddy hated. In very Lincoln-esque terms, Teddy said that wealth "must subserve the public good. We draw the line against misconduct, not against wealth."

Lincoln never stooped to name-calling or to assigning evil to individual people. Lincoln had the spirit of an eagle, and he had the heart and the mind of a good person. He was like an eagle, but he was better.

And with such power and scope we, too, can live in honor—down to the latest generation.

# 29

# We the People

*"Fellow-citizens, we cannot escape history."*

**-Abraham Lincoln**

http://bit.ly/2jBfnTm

**THE QUOTE ABOVE** is the opening line of Lincoln's final paragraph in a message to the Congress that he hoped would help him restore the country. It was December 1, 1862.

"Fellow-citizens, we cannot escape history" is the first of the final 13 sentences of this long address to Congress. In those 13 sentences, Lincoln uses the plural pronouns "we" and "us" 16 times. He truly believes in America as "We the people"!

We know that, historically, Lincoln is the politician, prophet and poet promoting the idea of democracy. For him, American life is about *we*, not *me*. We are tapping into the spiritual life of Lincoln when we reflect that democracy—this innovative, "we" form of self-government—meant everything to him. Wanting to make sure that Congress understood his point, he underscored the word "we" at the beginning of this closing paragraph.

Yet we can become jaded about such claims, can't we? So often in spiritual teaching and in religious life we hear that "we" is so much more important than "me." Many people in the 21st century are rejecting religion because there seems to be no room for "me"—for a personal sense of self.

Lincoln clearly had a personal sense of self, and he certainly did not intend that his plural and democratic way would erase his singular and personal self. In fact, one reason why he loved democracy was because it prevented a despot, a dictator, from taking over. His father had behaved in this manner when Lincoln was a boy. His father was a hard man, and Lincoln once said, about his youth, that "I felt like a slave."

Lincoln continues to be for us a person of many paradoxes, and one paradox is his balancing of a sense of the value of "we, we together" and his sense of "me, I"; of one's own power and responsibility. His law partner noted that Lincoln had great ambition, and his ambition was like a little engine—always running.

Lincoln is a practical role model for those of us who seek a spiritual balance between our personal selves and our social selves.

Not too many miles from where Lincoln grew up, Thomas Merton's spiritual voice arose just after World War II. Merton was a monk at the Gethsemani Trappist monastery in Kentucky, and he caught the world's attention with his memoir, *The Seven Storey Mountain*. In the 70 books that followed, Merton argued repeatedly against the "me, me, me" culture that arose in the 1950s and 1960s—especially among trendy religious leaders, whom he once dismissed as "a mild confabulation of clerical hippies."

Merton taught that real freedom comes from being set free from "monumental self-awareness" and "inordinate self-consciousness." He believed that life "in the Spirit" could deliver us from "the obsessions of a culture that thrives on the stimulation and exploitation of egocentric desire." He became fascinated with the wisdom Buddhism could bring to his Catholicism.

Lincoln, of course, knew nothing about the specific spiritual trends Merton was addressing a century after the Civil War. But we can recognize this theme of not-"me"-ness, of real selflessness, in Lincoln as he emptied himself into the cause of democracy and the celebration of freedom.

There is large painting of Lincoln that used to hang in a restaurant in Cape May, New Jersey. In it, Lincoln is a dark silhouette, recognizable only from the shadow of his iconic profile. Behind him is a huge red circle, perhaps like a gigantic rising or setting sun—but really just a big red circle that many would recognize from Buddhist meditation rooms. The image suggests that the unbounded ego of the enlightened self somehow sheds light on the boundless person that Lincoln became while serving America.

That circle of light can, as Lincoln said of those of us who embrace the responsibility of history, light us down in honor—to the latest generation.

# 30

# Lingering with Lincoln

*"People linger at the Lincoln Memorial."*

http://bit.ly/2jCX4NB

**THE QUOTE ABOVE** is what Dr. Wayne Baker, professor and friend of mine observed when he, his wife and young son visited the Lincoln monument in Washington, D.C.—that people mill around, walk slowly out and walk back in.

He added, "It's as if they don't want to leave."

Maybe you've been there. Maybe you've felt that way, too. It is very quiet at the Lincoln Memorial, inside those columns and walls.

Could this pull to remain in that space be proof that Abraham Lincoln was simply the real deal—that we know there wasn't a fake bone in his body? Of course, his views on race, government or even God might not be all we want for now. We also know that he brought politics near to our ideals. As we like to say, he "walked his talk."

Lincoln had an almost mystical sense of "the people." Remember those words: government of the people, by the people, for the people? That's a beautiful circle—of, by and for. He was, with his words, weaving a web of connection.

He called it *union*.

I think we trust that honest calling to this day. Lincoln was a common man, and most of us are common, too—and we want what is good for the commonwealth, as well as to be included in that. It's a real and spiritual pull that we feel.

Union. Communion. We really don't want to live in a divided house.

So maybe that big, white, marble cube of the Lincoln Memorial—spacious, silent, and spiritual—provides moments of sanctuary for us, the visitors, the tourists.

And so we linger.

There's another place in Washington, D.C. where people are drawn to Abraham Lincoln—where they almost cling to him—but not everybody knows about it. In the National Cathedral, in the right back corner, there stands an almost-actual-size, full-standing statue of Lincoln on a pedestal. It's called the Hancock statue. It is remarkable, partly because Lincoln is draped in his famous shawl. The statue is made of bronze. Lincoln's head seems tilted down a bit as you look up, and his right arm is extended. People have instinctively reached up and touched Lincoln's fingertips—so they are, of course, shiny from being stroked so often, like new copper (Lincoln!) pennies.

The spiritual life of Abraham Lincoln is now as much about our spiritual life as it is about his. Abraham Lincoln was a spiritual man, and we can be drawn to linger and to touch his spirit—down to the latest generation.

# Care to Learn More?

**TODAY, ABRAHAM LINCOLN** is as close as your smartphone, computer, TV—or any other device that can stream the countless eBooks, videos and even music related to Lincoln's life and legacy. If you prefer traditional ink on paper, your local library stocks many of the dozens of books I recommend.

Consider traveling, as well. There's so much you can learn—and feel— by walking where Lincoln lived. There are Lincoln locations spread across the eastern United States. A million people visit Gettysburg each year. The National Park Service maintains an online hub for five of the Lincoln sites at https://www.nps.gov/people/abraham-lincoln.htm. However, that website is certainly not exhaustive. Lincoln shows up in surprising corners of the U.S. Among my favorites is the bronze sculpture of him at the rear of the National Cathedral in Washington D.C. by Walter Hancock of Massachusetts. Visitors love to touch Lincoln's outstretched fingers and his boot, keeping them alive with a well-polished glow.

Here are some other Lincoln touchstones.

## Carl Sandburg

Whether you choose his original multi-volume version, or one of the condensations, don't be afraid to immerse yourself in his classic portrait of Lincoln. Although the poet won the 1940 Pulitzer Prize for History, his work has been criticized by historians as more of a literary impression of Lincoln's life rather than original research. Sandburg's defense was that he wanted to produce an American epic, perhaps a modern-day Iliad. He was right; there are few more evocative stories of great American heroes.

## Lincoln at the Movies

Lincoln is mythic, so movies are a perfect medium to summon his spirit. You can probably name your own favorites. My first memorable movie impression of Lincoln was toward the end of the 1957 melodrama *Raintree Country*, starring Elizabeth Taylor as a southern woman crazed with racial guilt. In a final sequence, we see the Lincoln funeral train winding its way back across the nation. This was an incipient image for me, conveying on screen what I later learned from reading Walt Whitman—that Lincoln was our "first Martyr Chief" and so his death is a grief that can unite us.

Don't overlook John Ford's 1939 *Young Mr. Lincoln*, which uses images of the river twice to illustrate the Lincoln who both loved women (his mothers and Ann and Mary) and the history that flowed from love. The Criterion Collection has issued a gorgeous new version of the movie for home viewing.

## Lincoln in Fiction

Why fiction? Any study of Lincoln soon leads to the awareness that he is larger than life, the very definition of fiction. That's how George Saunders won the 2017 Man Booker Prize for his *Lincoln in the Bardo*. The novel draws on Buddhist spirituality envisioning a free-flowing mingling of spirits after death. It's a great way to explore Lincoln's deep love and grief for his dead son.

Saunders certainly was not alone in claiming such literary license. The popular Scottish novelist John Buchan—more famous for a novel and later an Alfred Hitchcock movie called *The 39 Steps*—also published a fanciful cycle of stories called *The Path of the King* in 1921. At the core of Buchan's stories was a golden artifact that moved through generations of European rulers to wind up on the western edge of Kentucky in the hands of a young

Nancy Hanks. She gives it to her son Abraham. Buchan's novel again ends with Lincoln's death. Watching the funeral cortege, one character says, "There goes the first American." His friend replies, "But I think it is also the last of the Kings."

Consider for a moment that, when Buchan released his novel, some of the people who actually saw Lincoln's cortege—perhaps as children— were still alive. A century after that, such memories of Lincoln and loss were every bit as potent for Saunders' readers.

The Lincoln narrative certainly is larger than life!

## Dimensions of Psychology

Many writers who approached Lincoln have described a sometimes inspiring and sometimes unsettling experience of feeling Lincoln near them as they worked. When the scholar Mark Van Doren wrote the play *The Last Days of Lincoln* in 1959, he said, "I could hear Lincoln talking. I could almost hear him thinking."

Where fiction leaves off—psychology can open new doors. Joshua Wolf Shenk takes on the meaning and power of Lincoln's sadness in "Lincoln's Melancholy: How Depression Challenged A President and Fueled His Greatness." He writes, "What distinguished Lincoln was his willingness to cry out to the heavens in pain and despair, and then turn, humbly and determinedly, to the work that lay before him."

Others I can recommend in this genre include: *The Inner World of Abraham Lincoln* by Michael Burlingame; *Lincoln's Youth* by Louis A. Warren; and *Walt Whitman's Civil War*, a collection edited by Walter Lowenfels.

## Looking at Lincoln

Simply looking into Lincoln's face has inspired millions of men and women over the past century. Because his life coincided with the birth of modern photography, we have a wide array of images that are spread across the Internet.

For the opening of this book, I chose the famous cracked portrait, which was widely regarded as the last photograph of Lincoln before his death. For years, that made sense. The photo was taken by the famous Civil War photographer Alexander Gardner, who had photographed him seven times during his life. Later, Gardner would document his funeral, make portraits of the conspirators in the assassination plot and was the only photographer allowed at the site of their execution. However, historians later proved that Gardner's cracked plate was made two months before the president's death and other photographers had access to Lincoln after Gardner.

Nevertheless, I love this image, forever scarred by the dark line of the accidentally broken plate. That image foreshadows so much that would unfold for Lincoln and our nation.

# Lincoln's Own Words

Lincoln still speaks for himself.

Fred Kaplan's rich and detailed book *Lincoln: The Biography of a Writer* shows Lincoln's mastery with words. As Kaplan's Lincoln looks in the mirror—he almost sees Shakespeare, or Byron, or Burns.

In the book *Lincoln's Virtue: An Ethical Biography*, William Lee Miller's Lincoln looks in the mirror and sees more of the honor and political virtue of George Washington.

One often-overlooked reflection on the language of Lincoln was penned by Daniel Kilham Dodge. In the 1870s, Dodge left New York City with a doctorate from Columbia to chair the new English department at the University of Illinois, which had 714 students at the time. Dodge saw Lincoln not as a western pioneer but as the self-educated and cultivated product of the classics of English literature. To Dodge, Lincoln was a role model for any frontier student. He wrote his book hoping that western students would emulate Lincoln in *The Evolution of His Literary Style*.

A more contemporary wordsmith on Lincoln is Garry Wills. His pivotal 1992 book *Lincoln at Gettysburg: The Words that Remade America* makes the transition from Lincoln's secular talents to sacred wisdom. Lincoln "came to change the world, to effect an intellectual revolution. No other words could have done it," Wills writes. "He wove a spell that has not, yet, been broken—he called up a new nation out of the blood and trauma."

Using this literary analysis to illuminate Lincoln's spiritual life is historian Allen C. Guelzo in his 1999 *Redeemer President*. Guelzo won't call Lincoln a prophet, and certainly not a converted believer. However, Guelzo does explore how Lincoln felt he was contending with God's Will. Guelzo's research is so widely respected by his peers that, in 2009, Oxford University Press invited him to write the volume in Oxford's ongoing "A Very Short Introduction" series called simply: *LINCOLN*.

## Other Authors and Books

Considering the thousands of volumes published about Lincoln, my recommendations could continue until they fill another book. So, let me leave you with short notes on some other gems you won't want to miss.

Any collection of books about Lincoln's spiritual life should include Elton Trueblood's 1973 classic, *Abraham Lincoln: Theologian of American Anguish*. That book went out of print until Nancy Reagan mentioned it in Good Housekeeping magazine. A new edition of Trueblood's book was released by HarperOne with a different subtitle: "Lessons in Spiritual Leadership."

For another perspective from a self-identified Christian writer, take a look at Stephen Mansfield's *Lincoln's Battle with God: A President's Struggle with Faith and What It Meant for America*.

Some good books vanish from libraries over the decades. One book that was influential to me many years ago in graduate school—but now is hard to find: William J. Wolf's *Lincoln's Religion*. His book remains a milestone in this field. As a student, I was thrilled to find a scholar who regarded this as a viable topic for research. Wolf describes Lincoln as like a "biblical prophet" who saw himself as "an instrument of God" to a nation of God's "almost chosen people."

Then, for the record: I think the best Lincoln biographies are Benjamin Thomas's *Lincoln* as well as the classics by David Herbert Donald and Ronald C. White Jr. White also studies Lincoln's language and its religious qualities in *The Eloquent President*.

Also among the exceptional works in the field is *Lincoln's Tragic Pragmatism* by John Burt, which has the depth of Torah study as Burt analyzes the language, logic and values of Lincoln as a moral man in an immoral society. Burt brings expertise in all three salient fields: He is an English professor, he has encyclopedic knowledge of the relevant history and political philosophy, and he is a spiritually focused person in his Unitarian Universalist congregation.

Other highly respected volumes are *The Age of Lincoln* by Orville Vernon Burton, Kenneth J. Winkle's *The Rise of Lincoln: The Young Eagle* and, of course, *Team of Rivals* by Doris Kerns Godwin.

If you feel I have overlooked an essential recommendation, please contact me through the publishing house. Even as this book is published, I continue to travel, teach and write about Lincoln. I appreciate hearing from readers with thoughtful questions and insights. I can also be reached at Duncan.Newcomer@gmail.com.

***Duncan Newcomer and the Front Edge Publishing team, Autumn 2019***

# About the Authors: Duncan Newcomer and Abraham Lincoln

**THE FIRST TIME** I walked the land of Lincoln's boyhood home in southern Indiana, a place called Pigeon Creek, I had the intense feeling that his sheer personal goodness was still in the air. The spirit, or poetry, of that perception was, in a way, mundane and material—no great apparitions or images. I just felt that in the air, around the leaves of the trees and hidden in the rough bushes, there was a vestige of Lincoln's personal goodness. I had the passing hope that this spirit-in-the-air might rub off on me, but mainly I felt convinced that it followed him wherever—yes, *wherever*—he went throughout his life. From my own

THE AUTHORS, 1969.

religious tradition, I thought of Jesus being baptized in the Jordan River; of the Holy Spirit, in the form of a dove; and of the voice of the Father, descending upon Jesus in deep blessing. I felt then a theological, mystical conclusion: Certain people carry with them a concentration of some spirit that actually affects people around them and lasts beyond their lifetime. I thought, too, of Gandhi and the Buddha. That was my experience that summer day.

I have been carrying Lincoln around with me, as many people do, for decades. As a teacher, his education has been of theoretical interest to me. As a psychotherapist and family counselor, his psychological development and family relationships have informed my work and my view of my own, personal development. As a minister and preacher, Lincoln's theology and near-sermon speeches have been both intellectually challenging and revealing of the meaning of personal and national history. As a poet and writer, his literary achievements and interests have inspired me.

A person who likes Lincoln needs to be humble because so many people like him—even love him. Each of us takes our interest intensely and personally, as if he is somehow our own. Marilyn Monroe told Carl Sandburg, I have read, that she wished Abraham Lincoln had been her father. Leo Tolstoy knew enough about Lincoln that he esteemed him as the greatest of leaders, largely due to his Christ-like nature in teaching love for the enemy.

Many historians who write about Lincoln have a professional religious or theological background.

John Burt, author of the monumental and profound literary criticism and philosophical history of the Lincoln-Douglas debates, authored *Lincoln's Tragic Pragmatism*; he is an active member of the Unitarian-Universalist church and lists his sermons as well as his books and articles on his academic website.

Allen C. Guelzo, director of the Civil War Era Studies program at Gettysburg College, has a degree in biblical studies and a master's in divinity; he is a highly respected preacher, as well as a scholar of great renown, and he is author of a biography entitled *Abraham Lincoln, Redeemer President*. He is also a significant contributor to the studies and publication of 18th-century American theologian Jonathan Edwards.

Indiana historian Louis A. Warren, who estimated that he gave 3,500 speeches on Lincoln to over 1 million people during his long life, was an ordained Disciples of Christ minister.

Ronald C. White, author of many books on Lincoln—including the popular biography *A. Lincoln*—has been a theology professor at San Francisco Theological Seminary and Princeton Theological Seminary, with a Ph.D. in religion and history from Princeton University.

Benjamin Thomas, who started out in newspaper and museum work, joined the First Presbyterian Church in Springfield that the Lincolns attended and had a stepfather who was a Baptist minister. Thomas once said, on the Edward R. Murrow television show, *This I Believe*, that "through study of Lincoln I found beliefs I could cling to."

Gabor Boritt, former director of the Civil War Institute at Gettysburg College, has a book, *The Gettysburg Gospel: The Speech Nobody Knows*.

Garry Wills writes on religious themes, but has kept his Lincoln writing largely secular.

There are others, of course, with totally secular views and backgrounds.

One may think of Albert Beveridge, author of a major two-volume history of Lincoln but who was very respectful of the book *The Soul of Lincoln*, by the Rev. William E. Barton of the First Congregational Church in Illinois.

David Herbert Donald and Doris Kearns Godwin seem solely secular in their admiration and writing.

Fred Kaplan's *Lincoln: The Biography of a Writer* reveals the literary and intellectual Lincoln as no other book has, and goes out of his way to remove from his biography—even from the second Inaugural Address—any hint of transcendent thought or theology.

It is because of, and not despite, all of these thinkers and lovers of Lincoln—both secular and quasi-religious—that I write. My own writing on Lincoln began in the summer of 1970, as I tended children and the garden at the Edmund Sloane Coffin estate at Beaver Dam Stock Farm, on Long Island. While there, I wrote my master's thesis for the Union Theological Seminary in New York City, entitled, *The Education of Abraham Lincoln*. I took my title from Henry Adams' *The Education of Henry Adams*, which hardly ever mentions Harvard. My idea was to explode the concept of education. I wanted, in the late 1960s, to take the definition of education beyond schooling and into the process of submerging oneself in language itself; to explore education in terms of the philosophical and psychological process of acquiring language. The language of Lincoln then led me to the second theme in the thesis: that prophetic theology, and even Gospel-inspired politics, can be done—and, in fact, were done, by Lincoln—a non-professing, Enlightenment-thinking, rational humanist.

It is, then, into the hybrid field of the secular religious that I place Lincoln. I have found no better term for it than *secular religious*. It is a view of Lincoln that fits the "religion without religion" of the deconstructionist thinkers, such as Jacques Derrida and John Caputo at Syracuse University. I rest my case ultimately on the well-known fact that Lincoln himself was a bundle of contradictions: comic-tragic, active-passive, eloquent-silent, ebullient-melancholy and even feminine-masculine. If he can be—and he was—all those things, then he can be secular and religious as well.

I have carried the original concepts of that thesis around with me through four careers: teacher, therapist, preacher and writer. I have also brought with me, through my life, a large painting of Lincoln that I had commissioned in 1966 by David K. Stone, future president of the American Society of Illustrators. It is one of the few paintings (or pictures) of Lincoln standing. Its mysterious oil image portrays the haunting look of his face in those last few months before his death.

Mystery is the final concept in understanding the advent and development of Lincoln. No one can fully explain how he came to be who he was. No field of investigation can explain sufficiently why he was able to do what he did, how it was possible for him to do what seemed so fundamentally impossible—much less how he ended up in a position to do all those things.

John Philip Newell introduces his book, *Shakespeare, the Human Mystery,* writing, "What cannot be said about each one of us is always greater than anything that can be said." Or, as Shakespeare wrote in *1 Henry VI*:

> …what you see is but the smallest part…

> Were the whole frame here,

> It is such a spacious lofty pitch

> Your roof were not sufficient to contain't.

I thank my partner, Rebecca Jessup, Latin teacher and poet, for the insight that Lincoln reminds her of Joan of Arc. How, in other words, do we explain that such an unlikely person—in all ways—could have come into existence and have done, in real history, what they did?

Mark Twain took 12 years to write his biography of Joan of Arc. He thought it was his best (and also his favorite) book. In his massive research and many pages, he never gets beyond his original astonishment at her very being—and he is almost worshipful at the end.

What came to me during my first walk on the Indiana boyhood home grounds was

DUNCAN NEWCOMER IS SITTING NEXT TO THE SAME LAMP, DESK AND PORTRAIT.

my original astonishment at Lincoln's palpable and good presence; a worshipful feeling that he came to be what he became—and, moreover, that he came to be at all.

DUNCAN NEWCOMER, Autumn 2019

# Acknowledgments

**LINCOLN BELONGS TO** the ages and to the angels. To be honest, any book featuring Lincoln emerges from the historical past and from the spiritual beyond. My acknowledgments and thanks for this book, then, could go on and on.

It is certainly fitting that these mediations come to you now from the generativity of a community radio station. WERU 88.9 FM, on the coast of Maine, boasts that it is the voice of the people; the voice of the voiceless. This book also comes to you from the visionary publishing work of David Crumm and the community of dedicated people, including William Bode, an early fan of the book, at Front Edge Publishing, in Michigan, and the Read The Spirit online magazine.

Lincoln was not a self-made man, and this is not a self-made book. Lincoln did, as historian Kenneth J. Winkle concluded, chart the winds and set his wings so that, as a young eagle, he was lifted by the unique currents of America during his lifetime. He had an extraordinary spirit, of course, and that is the life of this book.

Union Theological Seminary in New York and professors Dwayne Huebner, Robert Wood Lynn and Robert Handy were the first to help me shape my lifelong love of Lincoln into a philosophy and a language about his religion and education. Clergy and professional friends—especially the Rev. Eileen Sypher—have, through the years, helped me to believe I was on to something regarding Lincoln as a secular and a sacred person.

Wayne Baker, from the University of Michigan—and from his perch as a values writer for Read The Spirit—was the first to welcome my writings into the new age of mass communication. One day, I sent out an emailed

SOS from near Lincoln's boyhood home in Indiana, saying to the computer gods: *Does anybody care about Lincoln and religion?* And Wayne Baker and David Crumm said, "Send us your stuff."

But what would a secular, community radio station want with the spiritual life of Lincoln? Did he even have a spiritual life? What could liberal progressives more open to Buddhism than patriotism want with an American president from the past? What could globally minded, ecologically active hippies and radical millennials want with religious and psychological words about history, war and politics?

When this feature started, four years ago, who cared about the character of a president? Obama was the gold standard and the future belonged to his legacy. Racism was more in the past than the present, and the community that mattered was the small colony of the saved that surrounded our radio transmission towers and the global village of the new world—certainly not national tribal identity.

Could a Calvinistic Protestant from the Enlightenment side of American politics really have anything to say to organic farmers, fishermen and artists, communities of poets and pent-up millennials?

To our collective astonishment—yes. We found a welcoming audience.

My thanks go mostly, of course, to my ultimate love and partner, Rebecca Jessup, who loves me and believes in me. To my sister, Beclee Wilson, and her husband, John, who have come to the same conclusion. To the friends who read my emailed versions of these talks: Jeff Byrum, Dave Edgerton, Peter Stevens, Bill Bonvillian.

The community of Belfast, Maine: the bookstores, the Old Professor's Book Shop, George Cisco, the Shop Talks, the Athenaeum, Senior College, the library, Brenda Harrington, the historical society, Megan Pinette, the churches and clergy—all have given me a "yes" for what I have to say about Lincoln, his spiritual life and his relevance to us today.

With your collective encouragement, I gratefully move radio conversations into the enduring form of a book.

Thank you, all.